ESCAPING UGLY

Overcoming Trauma to
Move From Surviving to Thriving

Deloris C. Gardner (SSWIR)

Escaping Ugly: Overcoming Trauma to Move from Surviving to Thriving
Copyright © 2021 Deloris C Gardner

ISBN: 978-1-77277-418-4

All rights reserved. No portion of this book may be reproduced mechanically, electronically, or by any other means, including photocopying, without permission of the publisher or author except in the case of brief quotations embodied in critical articles and reviews. It is illegal to copy this book, post it to a website, or distribute it by any other means without permission from the publisher or author.

Limits of Liability and Disclaimer of Warranty
The author and publisher shall not be liable for your misuse of the enclosed material. This book is strictly for informational and educational purposes only.

Warning – Disclaimer
The purpose of this book is to educate and entertain. The author and/or publisher do not guarantee that anyone following these techniques, suggestions, tips, ideas, or strategies will become successful. The author and/or publisher shall have neither liability nor responsibility to anyone with respect to any loss or damage caused, or alleged to be caused, directly or indirectly by the information contained in this book.

Publisher
10-10-10 Publishing
Markham, ON   Canada

Printed in Canada and the United States of America

Table of Contents

Acknowledgements	v
Foreword	vii
Introduction	ix
Chapter 1: Getting Rid of Self-Blame (Flip the Script)	1
Chapter 2: Practice Self-Resilience	13
Chapter 3: Practice Gratitude and Contentment	25
Chapter 4: Accessing Resources, Internal or External	37
Chapter 5: Controlling Triggers	49
Chapter 6: Own Your Box	61
Chapter 7: What We Can Learn from COVID-19	73
Chapter 8: Acceptance — The First Stage of Healing	85
Chapter 9: Avoid Familiarity and Opt for Change in Any Relationships	97
Chapter 10: Trauma Recovery	109
About the Author	121

ACKNOWLEDGEMENTS

Escaping Ugly is dedicated to all survivors of trauma in any forms; you are the real hero in your beautiful story.

My enduring gratitude is extended to:

God, for without him this book would never have been possible. There were many times I felt like giving up the idea of writing this book, but he has always been a constant source of strength in the darkest periods of my life.

My mother, Joslyn Humphrey, who quickly agreed with the idea of this book and is waiting with both fingers crossed to be the first to purchase a copy. I am living this dream through her eyes.

To all my siblings, thank you for your support, prayers and encouragement.

The remaining members of my family; this victory is for all of us. My niece Kiha for her support and guidance and for her patience listening to my many rumblings at the early stages of this book and checked in often to see how it was progressing.

My children, Caffi and Keeme, who supported me with my out of whack schedule which usually included long nights and even longer mornings. They never complained. They were just as anxious to see this dream come to fruition as I was. Caffi was and still is my biggest critic. She never gives me an easy pass, but keeps me on my toes.

My friend and former neighbor, David Spencer, and former Antigua & Barbuda Ambassador to China, Anthony "Mamba" Liverpool, for their support and encouragement. They were the trailblazers who saw the gift of writing and helped me to harness this skill.

My college professors, Philip Ackerman and Dr. Roohullah Shabon, who has left a lasting impression on my approach to the use of words.

My publisher Raymond Aaron and his staff of dedicated workers for making my vision a reality. The 10-10-10 program is a simplified version of exactly what I needed to start and complete this journey.

In 2004, Clephane "Terrific" Roberts, along with Mr. Barnes, opened his home at Side Hill to accommodate a group of "misfits" who were searching for something deeper and more meaningful in life. One of our many activities was goal setting. Each participant was asked to create a vision board. I entitled my vision board "More for 2004." That year almost everything on my vision board was accomplished just as I envisioned. I was fearless about what I wanted to accomplish, and was also specific. Mr. Roberts always said, "If you want to be dynamic you have to be specific." We had many success stories along the way, and this helped in igniting the fire in the heart of each participant. This was not due to luck, but through the teachings of Clephane and Mr. Barnes, with the help of God. The success of this book is for all the members of the Side Hill vision group. Special mention to my friends Pam and Kevin Armstrong, who were motivated to expand their business, and are now living in the US.

My dear friends, Antoniette Thomas and Makesa Greene-Cole, who are my spiritual sisters. They have helped me to be my authentic self and are fully accepting of whatever I bring to the table, even if it is nothing. These women keep me prayed up. Even if we are not living in the same country, they can sense when something is wrong and start the process of praying right away.

Finally, I would like to acknowledge my grandmother, Luenda Jobe-Cain (RIP). For many years I was bitter and had more questions than answers. She herself came from a cycle of abuse, and so it continued and disrupted the lives of many individuals in my family. I am not sure, if she were alive today, what her opinion of this book might be. What I would have wanted her to know is I have forgiven her, and thank her for bringing out this passion in me.

Lastly, may everyone reading the pages of this book find peace and hope. If there is anyone you must forgive, do it now.

FOREWORD

Have you ever experienced trauma? Do you feel immobilized as a result?

No matter who you are or what your current situation is, regardless of your age, culture, beliefs or religion, this book is full of insights and will act as guide in your life, teaching you how to move from surviving to thriving, while fulfilling your purpose. Trauma can form a thick cloud that can block the blessings God has in store for you, but with the right tools and an inner determination you can weather any storm.

I had the privilege of meeting Deloris at one of my writing workshops in the fall of November 2019. She stood out as someone who had a great story to tell the world, and she quickly started the journey to becoming a published author. In Escaping Ugly, Deloris shares with you her personal experience, and her journey from surviving to thriving, so they can be a catalyst on which you can make a blueprint for the rest of your life.

I am proud of Deloris, and what she has been able to accomplish this far, and I believe that the same is possible for you! If you are looking for a book that will challenge you to overcome your biggest setback while tapping into something greater than yourself, I highly recommend this book!

Raymond Aaron
New York Times Bestselling Author

INTRODUCTION

The word trauma is Greek for "injury or wound." The experience causes an injury to our brains that affects our emotional and intellectual functioning and, based on the severity of the trauma or the injury to the brain, the after-effect can range from mild to extreme, a state which would require some form of external intervention.

Trauma refers to an event or series of events that are highly threatening, and that lead to feelings of fear, helplessness, and horror. The events in our lives, especially in our childhood, have a huge impact on our mental health and wellbeing. Some of the most difficult experiences are called traumas. The issue of trauma has become a household name and is not necessarily classified as a singular event.

The most recent experience with COVID-19 is a reminder that we are all experiencing a collective form of trauma. Everyone is now gaining an understanding of trauma and its effect on humanity. We should now be working together as a people to become more empathic towards each other. We should strive to become our brother's keeper. Trauma has affected many lives, and unfortunately many have resorted to suicide, due to the many stigmas associated with those who may have expressed their own experiences.

When you have experienced a traumatic event, you may not feel the effects right away. But years later you may begin having thoughts, nightmares or other disturbing symptoms and not even remember the traumatic thing or things that once happened to you. Sometimes this is overlooked because you might have labelled it as a possible cause of depression, anxiety, phobias, or even being out of touch with reality.

Escaping Ugly: Overcoming Trauma to Move from Surviving to Thriving is a step by step guide to not only surviving your ordeal, but thriving. You are a product of your thoughts and intentions; if you fail to create an emotional balance then you are only robbing yourself of the keys to start the journey of healing. Many trauma survivors are stuck in "survivor mode" and may remain there for a long time. In this book I will show you how to heal the traumatized brain by moving from an individual approach to a collective approach. The book is written with the understanding that there are no one size fits all and so it is necessary to look at some areas that you may be having problems accepting. Like the title, trauma is often seen as something "ugly" and is not something that people are eager to talk about. But trauma doesn't have to be perceived as the worst chapter in your life story. Your trauma can be seen as your biggest blessing. It creates opportunities to start from a clean slate, and that can be a blessing in disguise.

I didn't allow trauma to dictate my future. You have that same power to decipher what you allow to control your mind, which can ultimately alter your future. My own experience with trauma is something that helped me to connect with my readers. My lived experience as a trauma survivor, as well as my background in social work, has helped me to gain a deep understanding of trauma and how it helps in shaping our thoughts and emotions. After my many experiences with trauma, I felt that my story was not meant to be shared but rather to be locked away in an archive, never to be looked at again. I was ashamed like you, but I want to remind you there is absolutely no shame in what you have experienced. Take complete ownership of it and let it become a huge part in shaping your future.

To embark on this mission, I had to first embrace my scars and use the broken pieces of my past to paint a beautiful picture of something more spectacular than what I had before. I hope you will embrace this book with an open mind, apply the tools within these pages, and create new techniques for yourself as you go along. See this book as your blueprint on the road to recovery.

I made the decision to escape the sea of sameness a long time ago, since my present reality was not reaping the benefits that I

Introduction

needed to feel whole again. I want to encourage you that all things are possible with the right mindset, and if you avail yourself of all available resources.

Happy reading. May you find peace, hope and joy on your journey to a better "YOU."

Chapter 1

Getting Rid of Self-Blame (Flip the Script)

When you are embarking on the path of getting rid of self-blame by flipping the script, developing an environment of being open-minded can reap many dividends. Open-mindedness is a positive character quality and it enables those who use it to think critically and rationally. By keeping an open mind, you are creating avenues to change your story. A closed mind does the opposite, of shifting your focus on "what did I do to deserve this" or "why me," to "what can I do to change my script." The question of "WHY ME" is going to become a regular occurrence in the early stages of the healing process, but there is no need to fear; it is okay. However, there are no answers in the "WHY ME," just self-pity, and this can go on for as long as you allow it. You have a choice in the way your script should be written after trauma. Giving self-pity a run for its money will open many doors for the healing process to take place.

You cannot undo the pages of your story; however, what you can do is to start a new page and write the final chapters of your life. Make it grand!! Let your bad experiences become your new voice, and live unapologetically without regrets. Bad situations can tend to throw us off course and can even threaten to change the course of our lives, developing the attitude of changing your story. Flipping the script is the same approach as killing a lion; it silences the naysayers and, most importantly, the perpetrator. This also acts as a motivation for you to take back your sense of self. Trauma is usually inflicted by a weak individual who is struggling with some form of inner demon, and they disguise their outer existence by preying on others. Over time, the perpetrator can become more violent because they may have the notion that they are unstoppable. In the "dead lion approach," the lion is powerful, but removing the power will render him powerless.

Taking back control of your life is the only way you can flip the script. It is not going to be an easy road ahead, because you have been manipulated into believing that you are a "nobody," and that you deserve what has been happening to you. Sad to say, you may even believe these negative sayings, and that is where the perpetrator derives their power from. They are scoring points in every department where you are concerned, and will continue their deadly game. After hearing this, over a period of time, you sadly adapt to their behavior and may unfortunately believe you deserve it. The longer you stay in any kind of relationship that degrades, humiliates, or threatens your existence, the more power you are giving to the offender, and most vital, the more your life is in danger.

Flipping the script is a psychological approach that allows the brain the do the work for you without doing any physical activity. It is slowly allowing you to work on your internal ability, and forming your character to become more resilient. After all, the work of restoration starts first with the mind, and eventually everything else would fall into place. The offender has manipulated not only your physical being but also your psychological being. They want you to believe that you are theirs whenever they want you, and that you are obligated to them on their terms. You may even feel like your body has betrayed you, since it moves by the forces of the offender's voice. When they are not around, your body becomes numb by your touch. You have become a prisoner in your own body. Help may even seem like a farfetched dream that ceases to exist, but always remember that "the forces of your inner being are greater than any outer forces!!" The great writer, Maya Angelou, said, "The quality of strength, lined with tenderness, is an unbeatable combination." You have the power to flip the script and change the course of your destiny by rewriting your story. Trauma has destroyed many lives, and if you are blessed enough to be an overcomer of trauma, like myself, then make your existence count—never live a day in your life with regrets, but be proud that you are a survivor, and wear your scars with pride.

Find the Giant in You

In the story of David and Goliath, we are reminded of a mere small boy defeating a giant. Everyone was afraid of the huge giant, but David didn't look at his small stature; he was depending on a force that was greater than him, to change the course of history. There is a giant in all of us; however, due to prolonged periods of abuse and neglect, we become brainwashed into believing that we are a "nobody." You have unconsciously made a choice to shrink your standards and throw your principles out the window to glorify others. Many people doubted David's abilities because the focus was on the outside, but with a mind fixed on a much greater inner force, David did the unthinkable. An insurmountable giant fell and died due to David's sheer determination. Conquer your fears and find the giant within you!!

The greatest form of control for the victim is to take back their power from the offender, which would render them powerless. The offender knows too well that they can't proceed any further without laying the foundation of manipulation and control. The extreme approach is to even resort to blackmail, where they demand secrecy, or they would hurt someone in your family. During these dark periods of pain, stay away from isolation, and develop the habit of speaking to someone you trust. Choose very wisely who that person is going to be, and don't take the "willy-nilly" approach. Never leave an abusive relationship and notify the offender; you may not live to tell the tale. Slowly make an escape plan and act on it once you are comfortable enough to proceed further. Studies have shown that a victim is more at risk nearing the break-up of a relationship or when the offender senses resistance.

Awakening the giant within you is the psychological approach that allows you to take back power and take back control of your life. You are more powerful than you believe; you are a force to be reckoned with. You can take a stand even when everything around you is crumbling; however, take strategic steps to free yourself from bondage. The longer you stay, the greater and more detrimental it would be for you.

Another and very vital area to focus on is raising your standards and changing your belief system. Nothing happens by chance; every bad thing that ever happened to you has been orchestrated by your offender. You sadly buy into the notion that this is going to be the last time; or in my case, it was a mistake and would never happen again. But years of abuse have made you immune to the pain, and you may sadly believe that it is your fault. Little David did the unthinkable when he defeated Goliath—you have that same power, but you need to tap into your inner source. You need to raise your standards and demand transparency; unleash the giant in you, and make wise decisions that would impact your life in a positive way. Once you have raised your standards and beliefs, never tolerate mediocracy from others. Finally, when you raise your standards, your perspective and perception of life changes for the better. It is important to note that your mind is a limitless source that has the power to propel your entire body, based on what you feed it. Be wise, find the giant in you, and work daily on becoming the person you have always wanted to be. Always remember that David only needed a small stone; tap into the limitless source of your mind to find that inner giant and change your story.

Forgive Yourself

After experiencing trauma, many people find it more difficult to forgive themselves; it is one of the most challenging tasks on your journey to healing. The effect of trauma not only affects your mental state, but it changes the way you think and feel about yourself. Breaking away and setting yourself free can prove to be one of the most difficult tasks you have ever embarked upon. Unforgiveness is like a slow death, where anger, resentment, stress, and even physical and psychological problems reside. Only in forgiveness can you break down these barriers and forge a new path. The sad reality is that the offender may have moved on with their lives, while you are wallowing in self-pity. Releasing yourself will slowly unlock the key to your liberation from trauma.

As humans, we are prone to making mistakes; it's inevitable once we are breathing. Freeing yourself will set you free from the bondage of your offender. Genuine forgiveness is not a sign of weakness; rather, it exemplifies strength and healing. Sometimes you may feel like it was your fault, but if you try to rethink it, you might find the truth. The offender has stolen many things from you; but in forgiveness, you are taking back the keys to navigate your ship into the harbor of peace and tranquility. Sometimes forgiveness seems like the hardest thing to do; but without forgiveness, you are locking yourself in a zone that will keep you there for as long as you allow it to. The pain of trauma can be the most unbearable pain anyone can experience, because it encompasses the physical, psychological, and emotional being. It interprets the way you function on a daily basis, sometimes to a severe degree where you may feel like a little baby trying to walk again for the first time.

Forgiveness can never replace what you have lost, or undo the wrongs. It would never take away the pain; however, what it does is allow you to look in the mirror and free yourself of self-hate. You may feel like what happened to you is not that simple and may not be so easy to erase, but with daily practice and much effort, you will accomplish your goal. Unforgiveness blocks your mind from learning the valuable lessons from your ordeal, but forgiveness opens the door to wisdom. Embrace the scars from your past, and wear them with pride, because that dark experience would become the bridge that would elevate you into a place of hope.

Rather than tormenting yourself with guilt and shame, having compassion for your own suffering can help you to achieve the clarity necessary for repairing the harm that was done against you. When someone experiences trauma, they become haunted by the event for a long time. Given the nature of what trauma sufferers have seen and experienced, this is understandable. Acts of violence, abuse, disaster, and war are absolutely abhorrent events for someone to live through. When someone experiences trauma of any form, they become haunted by these events and may experience consistent flashbacks and disruptions to regular sleep patterns. Flashbacks are common occurrences; it may feel like the trauma experience is happening again, but it is natural and would eventually go away with time. Don't be hard on yourself; you are entitled to these unexplained moments. Remember that you are entering your period of liberation, and only time will heal all wounds. After all, you are moving on from a dark place of hurt and pain, so find lessons of what you have learnt from your experience. It is important to allow the natural process of working through trauma to happen, and to remove any barriers that may get in the way. This includes the belief that we aren't supposed to feel "negative" emotions, or that we must forgive. Unforgiveness is the breeding ground of fear and unnecessary prolonged periods of emotional stress. Once we remove that expectation, the natural process moves through. Even if someone doesn't get to a place of forgiveness, he or she can still move on, unburden themselves, and thrive.

Healing the Traumatized Brain

Studies have shown that approximately 50% of the population may at some point have experienced trauma. The severity and length of trauma can have a negative impact on the function of the brain. Some damages may be difficult to repair; however, you can work on rewiring the brain tissues by learning skills that can pave the way for the recovery process to take place. In the re-traumatization stages of my trauma, my brain did a 360-degree spin on me; I was initially in shock, denial, and anger, and I would even experience all three at the same time. However, I had to face the reality of the situation. My world was at a standstill, and absolutely nothing, and no one, was making sense to me. I called it the "zombie stage"—I felt like I was going crazy. The severity of the damage to my brain brought on post-traumatic stress disorder (PTSD). The unique feature of the brain is its ability to change based on what we feed it; in other words, the brain is as flexible as plastic, and can adapt to the changes that are happening in our lives.

In a younger individual who may have experienced trauma, the brain can act as a protective mechanism to shield the magnitude of the trauma, by allowing the person to go into shock and remain in that state until it can differentiate when to process this information. Without this protective mechanism in place, the damage to the brain and the traumatized individual would have been detrimental; in other words, that person may have gone "over the edge." The road to recovery, and healing the traumatized brain, is going to take time and a willingness to be open-minded that there are no quick fixes in this area of change. Trauma can alter the functioning of the brain in many ways. However, the three most important to note are the changes that occur in the prefrontal cortex (PFC), also known as the "thinking center"; the anterior cingulate cortex (ACC), known as the "emotion regulation center"; and the amygdala, known as the "fear center." Fears are usually based on bad memories, and our brains are avoiding the repeated occurrences.

People who have experienced trauma may have noticed changes in their ability to focus and concentrate, and in loss of memory. You may even lose interest in the things you loved to do before the trauma happened. In addition, your emotions are running on high all the time, and you feel incapable of staying calm. Take deep breaths, and practice counting from 1–10 slowly. Because there is a breakdown in your emotional system, it is difficult to take control of what is happening around you. Healing the traumatized brain takes time and much effort, and the best gift you can give yourself is to seek help from a psychologist. The biggest fear, for many people who have experienced trauma, is that they may not be financially stable to afford a psychologist; and even worse, in the Caribbean, it is difficult to locate one. Help may seem like a dream for many people, and the huge bill that goes along with the healing process may be just as hard as coping with the trauma itself.

In the journey to healing, the good news is that changes in the brain can be reversed. There is no one-size-fits-all approach; the brain is complex, and finding a solution is based on an individualized approach and the severity of the trauma to the brain. A person who experienced PTSD after trauma, for example, may require more intensive care to repair the damaged tissues. PTSD is an anxiety disorder that can develop after exposure to any major events that have a negative impact on our lives. Another relevant thing to note is that the brain can repair itself with treatment and the right resources. After trauma, another gift you can give yourself is finding ways of availing yourself to whatever resources are out there to help you on your journey of repairing and healing your brain. Take baby steps, and treat every step as a journey to your success in healing your mind, body, and soul. It is written in Job 14:7, *"For there is hope of a tree, if it be cut down, that it will sprout again, and that the tender branch thereof will not cease."* Job knew that if a tree is cut down and uprooted, it has the chance to grow again. In trauma, you have been uprooted from your original foundation, but there is a bigger picture, and that is the example of Job in the Bible. When you have been uprooted, it is a new opportunity to start afresh, to grow and blossom into the flower you have always dreamed about.

The Practice of Mindfulness

While the effort of trauma creates stress on the brain, the practice of mindfulness meditation alleviates the damage of trauma with time. Mindfulness is a mental state achieved by focusing one's awareness on the present moment, while calmly acknowledging and accepting one's feelings, thoughts, and bodily sensations. It helps with trauma symptoms of reliving the past and remaining hypervigilant about potential threats. Due to the damage caused by trauma, mindfulness allows the brain to refocus, and helps you to live in the present moment. This is also used as a wonderful therapeutic technique. When you experience trauma, the "amygdala"—which is the brain's fear center—

sounds the alarm, and your body instinctively responds almost immediately with hormonal and physiological changes. That is where the term "fight or flight mode" comes from, because your brain is getting ready to run or do battle. Mindfulness helps to slowly restore your brain tissues.

Trauma disconnects you from the present, and you need help to refocus, which is where mindfulness comes into play. It is an asset for trauma survivors. In addition, it can enhance present moment awareness, increase self-compassion, and strengthen a person's ability to self-regulate—these are vital skills that can aid in the recovery process. Since the major effect of trauma may be a physical event, the reality is how the mind and body react to what happened. Although traumatic events have been shown to have a huge impact on a person's ability to function on a daily basis, not much is done to remedy the situation. In many countries, it is still taboo to seek out mental health care for those affected. Furthermore, some people are afraid of being stigmatized as being weak if they admit to feeling depressed or disoriented. This is a major contributing factor to an increased risk for deteriorating health and further damage to your overall health. Never succumb to such pressure from society, but rather avail yourself to whatever help is available. Furthermore, if you can't afford to see a psychologist, due to financial reasons, make the internet your friend by finding relevant resources.

It is important to note that the practice of mindfulness must not be taken lightly; in fact, it can be a double-edged sword if not used correctly. Mindfulness helps to nurture trauma survivors by increasing body awareness and encouraging emotional regulation, which are an integral part of trauma recovery. Make sure it is done in a setting where there is an awareness of trauma, since mindfulness can exacerbate trauma symptoms. It is imperative to pay close attention to the inner turmoil that people may be going through, since survivors may be experiencing emotional arousal, flashbacks, disassociation, and even re-traumatization. Refrain from practicing this on your own, especially in the early stages of trauma, but rather do this with the help of a professional coach. It is also advisable to embark on this journey when you are comfortable enough to emotionally deal with the issues.

Finding Beauty after Brokenness

We are living in a broken world. I am sure no one can dispute this statement; we don't have to look very hard at the events in our lives to ascertain this. We don't have to look very hard to become aware that we are living in a society that aches for peace, where there seems to only be turmoil. We long for a day when the sorrow and suffering is no more. To be hopeful is to look on the future positively, to see opportunity in your setbacks as opposed to challenges in opportunities. Always strive to look on the bright side of every situation. Hopefulness is the ability to not look at your current condition but be open to change, irrespective of your current outer condition. People often think that hopeful people are naive, even foolish, and that they believe good things will happen when in truth they never will.

Finding beauty after brokenness is an opportunity to reinvent yourself. You have gained insights into the past hurts and are now creating opportunities to start afresh. Many people believe, after trauma, that their life would be over, but God created an opportunity to start over. It is a myth for people to view brokenness as a negative or bad thing; however, brokenness symbolizes a dawn of a new era in your experience. Like the potter uses the clay after putting many broken pieces together, the end result is a beautiful creation. Make healing your number one priority in whatever steps you can muster, with the assurance that treasure will someday be found in the scars that the healing leaves behind.

The beauty in brokenness has a power unlike anything else, to bring forth fresh beauty, strength, and inspiration to others. It is only after you have tasted deep suffering that you become aware that you are made for more, and that there is a purpose even in your darkest moments. You have a story to share—the scars of the past, the healed wounds, all tell a story. We often try to hide away, preferring instead to present to the world a safe façade of who we are, with the notion that perfection is more acceptable from the world viewpoint. This is done to hide the risk of exposing our real vulnerability—but don't ever for a moment become fearful about your past. God specializes in putting the broken pieces of our lives together; he is a healer, a repairer, and he fits the broken pieces that no longer seem to fit, right into a perfect design.

Surviving a traumatic event can leave one feeling numb and cold hearted. After all, we shape our lives based on our experiences due to the severity and the damage of trauma. We tend to see our entire lives shaped by what happened, which left scars on our hearts and minds, and it becomes harder to find joy and enjoy life. Debilitating symptoms interfere with your daily life. In your season of brokenness, it is common to experience distressing thoughts, images, and feelings of hopelessness. These are common reactions and are signs that the body is recovering from severe stress. To heal from brokenness means that remembering the trauma stops terrifying you. For this to happen, you need to learn how to face your fears and be able to talk about what happened. Take slow but intentional steps, and increase sharing details of your ordeal. The aim is to face the fears and work on eliminating the terrible memories so that they no longer intrude in your life. Recovery is the primary goal to heal from brokenness; it does not necessarily mean complete freedom. It is an individual experience and will look different for everyone. In general, it is the ability to live in the present without being overwhelmed by the thoughts and feelings of the past. The main part of restoration of what is left after trauma, is empowerment to rebuild your future. Rise above the broken pieces of your life, and embrace the beauty of molding the pieces together and creating something beautiful.

"You may shoot me with your words, you may cut me with your eyes, you may kill me with your hatefulness, but still, like air, I'll rise!"
– Maya Angelou

Escaping Ugly

Notes

Chapter 2

Practice Self-Resilience

After trauma, life goes on; it is not waiting for us to get it together. Developing the practice of resilience is going to be a major factor in your capacity to recover quickly from difficulties. Working daily on self-improvement is going to pay you dividends on your journey to building a better you. Let's face it, life is already full of challenges and hardships; and to add insult to injury, you are facing further turmoil with the unfortunate issue of trauma. But always remember that you are not alone!! There is a community of support out there, and you need to work on building your community even if it is two people—this is vital. Most importantly, you must first embrace the will and desire to find your inner voice. In order to move forward, you need to develop the ability to tap into your inner strength. Hope is the key that fuels your emotion and ignites resilience deep in your soul, to not only cope but to purposely curve out a path and the desire and will to live and not give up. When I started my journey, I had a wonderful community of supportive individuals from diverse backgrounds, and so the diverse experiences played an integral part in my desire of becoming stronger. Before this, I thought of my past on an individual scale; but with the input of others, my focus was collectively on my community and all the greatness and possibilities that I found in these amazing ladies. They are truly awesome!!

I was always fascinated with the Holocaust and the Jews' determination and will to survive the death camps. In school, I had the great privilege of reading the book, *Night*, by Eli Wiesel. My life came to a complete halt because I realized that my experience of trauma is nothing compared to what his generation went through. We must build our mindset to believe that there is nothing insurmountable. Always look at the big picture and not only what we see at a glance. We can be deceived into believing that there is only one way of doing something, when in reality, if only we extend our thought pattern, we can see more. For example, you look at a mountain and, in your subconscious mind, all you see is a huge obstacle, and you immediately start thinking of the difficulties of climbing that mountain—but always remember that there are always other ways of overcoming your "mountain." Once we see that we can accomplish what we thought we couldn't, we are better prepared to embrace new challenges and opportunities.

I made some huge changes in my life after trauma, and many people may call it crazy or outrageous, but when you have gone to hell and back, you develop a certain quality of stubbornness to do what you want, regardless of obstacles. Change in any form took on a whole new meaning for me, and therefore I became more adaptable to change. With change comes a bigger responsibility to self; and regular introspection of where we are going and what path we are taking to get there is vital. Make wise decisions, and evaluate everything with a fine-tooth comb; be quick to dismiss any negative path, without regrets or shame. Resilience is to develop a unique quality of understanding: We can't undo the hands of time, but what we can do is to change ourselves to adopt to this new change.

Trauma is full of many unanswered questions, and it is okay not to know the answers—knowing the answers wouldn't make a difference in what you have experienced. *Man's Search for Meaning* is Viktor Frankl's remarkable memoir of surviving the Auschwitz death camp. He realized in Auschwitz that the difference between those who died in the death camp, and the survivors, was a combination of luck and a desire to live. Frankl wrote, "When a man knows the "why" to his existence, he will be able to bear almost any "how." Resilience puts the fire in your soul to fight on, even when everything around you is falling; it is training your mind to see hope amidst chaos. When you condition your mind to see beyond your current condition, you are planting the seed of resilience. You can smile during your storms, because happiness, resilience, and motivation are greatly increased when we have something to look forward to.

Reclaim Your Life

When I hear the word "trauma," I think of something ugly; hence, the reason for the book title. The experience is one of the hardest things a person can ever encounter, and the aftereffects can leave damages that you would carry with you for the rest of your life. Trauma hijacks your identity and takes away your most precious prized possession without your permission—things that you can never get back. There can be times of turmoil and pain, seasons of depression, and even suicide attempts, which God can prevent. I am a living testimony of this: I am alive because God kept me and never let me go, not even for a minute. If you have ever suffered from the effects of trauma in any form, whether it is domestic violence, illness, or trauma after the war, you are aware of the first sign of feeling disenfranchised from society and the person you used to be. Finding your true sense of self is an uphill battle; in fact, it is one of the hardest battles you may ever face. During your trauma, you were brainwashed into believing many negative things about yourself, and the many assaults on your body may validate the truths of what the offender has said. Everything around you may subconsciously remind you of this; your emotions, flashbacks, and triggers are all working against you. Reclaiming your life is to develop an understanding of who you are now, and to make a decision to determine who you want to be, going forward.

Look at the person you were before trauma, who you are after trauma, and who you want to become. Create a better version of yourself!! After trauma, I made the decision to go back to school; and honestly, I knew I was still facing the aftermath of trauma. I completed my studies as an honor student in Social Services; I took the journey to reinvent myself and never looked back. I am still in awe of my accomplishment, but I know I owe it all to God and some of the qualities I developed after trauma, which propelled me to strive for excellence. Anything is possible once you open your mind to make a change from your present situation to something better in the future. Many famous motivational speakers and celebrities have a story to tell that would resonate from the darkest moments of their lives. Their past is the driving force behind their successes. There are many unanswered questions, and "why" is where hope resides; it is a huge part of what motives us to hold firm to our dreams.

Plan for your life, and take steps toward reclaiming your life; starting over is not as bad as it seems. Create a recovery plan and build a solid foundation; mold it with your past experiences and imply new ideas. Eradicate "blame" from your vocabulary. You are entitled to have more bad days than good ones. Never feel shame for not being strong enough to protect yourself or those you love against violence or abuse. Leave the shame and blame to the offender of violence and those in society that did nothing to help. Society labels survivors of trauma as mentally ill, when it is their social conditions and the horrifying things that happened that are the real problems. This is the very reason why there is an increase in violence and abuse in society, since the victims are the ones that suffer the most. A huge aspect of reclaiming your life totally depends on you; the responsibility is in your hands. Work on the major parts of your body: the conscious mind, responsible for thoughts; the subconscious mind, responsible for feelings; and the body, responsible for action. All these parts make up our attitude, and our attitude determines the action and the result we want to see in the future. How you see yourself is how others see you. Never live another day in mediocracy; thrive above your setbacks, the difficulties, and the pain, and rise like the eagle and soar high above your past. Your purpose is bigger than you realized. You are destined to be limitless. Discover your true purpose by first reclaiming your life after trauma, and open the doors to greatness and miracles.

The Power of Journaling for Self-Reflection

Edward George Bulwer Lytton (1803–1873), an English novelist, coined these words in 1839: *"Beneath the rule of men entirely great, the pen is mightier than the sword."* The old proverb means that words are more powerful and effective than weapons in accomplishing your purpose. Putting your thoughts on paper is a vital form of healing from trauma. This can become a therapeutic tool that allows you to write down your thoughts daily. In addition, you can track your progress and create accountability for yourself. When we experience a traumatic event or major transition in life, our minds function to process and understand what's happening to us. Our thoughts can consume us, keeping us up at night or distracting our performance at work or school. By translating these experiences in words, it gives us a physical piece to contemplate, and therefore giving us better insights on what we experienced. In addition, the ability to construct a story from our experiences may give us the opportunity to detach ourselves and approach our situation more objectively. Stories may also be better stored in the brain as memories, rather than strong emotions. Whenever we consistently feed our minds with negative thoughts, we are putting our emotions at risk and creating feelings of overwhelm and hopelessness. Be cautious when documenting the horrible events; you may be triggered or have flashbacks, but think about the long-term benefits. By standing back every now and then, and evaluating your progress, it adds to your quality of life.

As Edward George Bulwer Lytton stated, there is power in words, and the ability to take strategic steps toward self recovery starts with you. The sword can symbolize your emotions, your past, or society—anything that is a barrier between you and the healing process must become subjective. Journaling helps by reducing body tension, restoring focus, assisting in organizing your thoughts, and enabling you to regulate your emotions. Journaling is one of the methods of helping people cope with any type of traumatic event. In addition, writing helps to add meaning to some of your unanswered questions, and helps to foster positive life changes following a traumatic event. Your preparation for journaling ensures that you have a gratitude journal as well, so as to keep a balance between the unpleasant memories and the good things in your life you are grateful for. Review your writing, and pay close attention to how you are feeling: Has your thought pattern changed as a result of your writing? Although writing is important, one must keep in mind that it is natural for old feelings to resurface, and you may experience distressing thoughts. Make sure you have a plan to regulate and manage these distressful feelings.

Be as specific as possible about your traumatic experience: how it made you feel, both physically and emotionally. What have you learned from this experience, and how does it make you feel? Brainstorm ideas on how you can transform your life by helping others. Seek out moments in your life to express gratitude. Gratitude creates a balance in your experience and is one of the most overlooked tools that we all have access to every day. According to research, practicing gratitude for a short amount of time can lead to higher levels of well-being. The practice of gratitude enhances empathy and reduces aggression. The word "gratitude" is derived from the Latin word "gratia," which means grace, graciousness, and gratefulness. Gratitude helps people feel more positive emotions, relish good experiences, and improve their health. It also helps with adversity and to build strong relationships. Finally, when you put your thoughts on paper and are implementing gratitude, you are transferring your power and anger, and putting it on paper. It is a monumental shift in focus to not be looking at what you don't have, but to be hopeful that everything will fall into place with time. Implementing a journal, and practicing gratitude on your journey to healing, can prove to be an asset over time.

Become Assertive

As a child, I grew up in the Caribbean, and many people believed in the notion that children should be seen and not heard; so in other words, you couldn't speak up for yourself or question an adult. This was the stick that broke the camel's back, because adults used it against children in every possible way to intimidate and control. If you dared to question an adult, you would be punished severely. When my abuse started, I tried to speak up but to no avail, and the pain was unbearable. For years, I believed that I was the reason for what was happening to me, and this further deepened when I had to fight the giants on my own—a mere child trying to be another "David the giant slayer" in modern times. I believed what my manipulators said about me, and this eventually led to anger and resentment. For years, I hated my body for betraying me, and my inner being was slowly dying a slow, painful death. So, embracing assertiveness initially felt like being hit by lightning, since all I had ever known in my life was to be passive-aggressive. The modern day "me" is a shadow of my formal self. I am very outspoken and independent, and I have a low tolerance for anything that threatens my peace. This is a symbol of growth, freedom, and self-compassion. I will no longer compromise my deepest values; I am learning daily to become my own best friend.

Learning to be assertive can help you set limits on the things you want to agree with and welcome in your life, all without draining your energy and/or neglecting to take care of yourself. Once you start exercising your ability to safeguard your inner peace at all cost, it will be the most refreshing feeling in the world and will boost your self-esteem. As in everything, there needs to be a balance. Assertiveness requires being forthright about your wants and needs; however, we should also consider the needs of others as well. We should practice fairness and empathy with ourselves and others. Furthermore, let us remember the golden rule: "Do unto others as we do unto ourselves." Treat others with dignity and respect, and we will get the same treatment in return.

Many survivors of trauma experience losses that can be tangible, like people we loved, or a body that once functioned perfectly. For others, the losses are intangible, like a sense of uncomplicated wholeness or pristine memories of beloved times and places. Either way, coming to terms with irreversible loss is an essential part of trauma integration and recovery. Fill in the missing pieces of your life after trauma, by using the tools that you have now; over time, you will acquire more. Assertiveness is one of the tools you can gain after trauma, but it is your decision to make, and there is absolutely no time frame; it is all up to you.

To stand up for yourself, you must be more assertive, but this can be tricky. You need to practice with someone you trust, until you have the confidence to try it in public. For many people, the thought of becoming assertive makes you feel uncomfortable because you have been conditioned for too long not to rock the boat, and to play it safe. But remember that you are taking a brave step to regulate your emotions and build your self-esteem. In a society that is changing at a rapid speed, the need to be assertive is a valuable tool that will improve your ability to become an effective communicator and negotiator. This famous quote by Shannon L. Alder sums up what assertiveness means: *"Staying silent is like a slow growing cancer to the soul, and a trait of a true coward."* There is nothing intelligent about not standing up for yourself. You may not win every battle. However, everyone will know what you stood for: "YOU." Remember, we are teaching people how to treat us by what we allow, and if we fail to set boundaries and avoid pleasing others, then we are laying the precedent for future relationships. People will respect you more in the end when you have structured your life where transparency is the order of the day, so that others know what you stand for.

Take Charge of Your Mind

My life changed the day I was fortunate enough to read the book, *Think and Grow Rich*, by Napoleon Hill. I began to understand the power of the mind and the power we possess to change the course of our destiny. I read this book for the first time in 2004; that year, I created a vision board for my life, and it is still the best success story to this day. We are sitting on a gold mine and don't even know it; we have the power to train our minds to work for us instead of against us. The law of life is that your outer world is merely a reflection of your inner world. Your biggest enemy is your mind—and why do I make that bold statement? Because we are not our minds; we are not the thoughts that come out of our minds. The many thoughts that bombard our minds every day are based to some degree on other people's opinions. So why should we believe everything it tells us? The mind can make us believe things about ourselves that are not true. Once you become aware of this information, it is the first step to total freedom. How many times have our minds made us believe something that is false? The mind acts as a protective mechanism to shield us from danger, but sometimes it can work against us by feeding fear to emotionally cripple us from progressing. Every problem starts in the mind; pay close attention to your conscious and unconscious mind, and to your body. The conscious mind is responsible for "thoughts"; the unconscious mind, "feelings"; and the body, "action." On your journey to healing, pay close attention to what your mind is telling you, and know you have the power to disassociate yourself from any negative thoughts that your mind is feeding you.

As a child, I can recall many episodes of silently screaming due to the many voices in my head telling me I can't do something. I would always reply with the comeback line: "I am going to prove you wrong." Our thoughts are like the laws of the universe, but our greatest power is choice: We can decide to allow or reject negative thoughts. For many years, I internalized the negative things that others said about me, and I unfortunately believed them to be gospel. It was not until I made the choice to decipher what I wanted to hear, and to disregard what I didn't, that I was able to make a change. Thought is powerful, but when it is mixed with purpose, it is unstoppable. We are the captains of our own ships, whereas in the past, we were victims to the vicious cycle of negative thoughts; but we can change the narrative by deciding to reject negative thoughts.

Experts estimate that the mind thinks between 60,000 and 80,000 thoughts per day. That is an average of 2500 to 3,300 thoughts per hour. The average person has about 48.6 thoughts per minute. These thoughts are based not only on your experiences but on your interactions with others, and what you see, smell, etc. But we have the power of choice to decide what we allow to be our outer existence and have dominance over our lives. Clear your mind from toxic thoughts. Just imagine for a minute that you had experienced trauma decades ago, and the negative comments from the offender, or people in society, are still tormenting you. When we try to change our thinking, we are actually taking steps to change our lives for the better. Quiet the silent critics in your mind that say you can't get ahead. You, and only you, are responsible to take a step to change your destiny, irrespective of your past. John Milton said, *"The mind is its own place, and in itself can make a heaven of hell, a hell of heaven."* May we allow God to guide our thoughts, heal our scars, and lighten the way that leads to total fulfillment. The famous Jamaican singer, Bob Marley, said, *"Emancipate yourselves from mental slavery; none but ourselves can free our minds."* Safeguard your mind, since out of it flows the issues of life. Evaluate each thought, exercise your greatest power—which is choice—and make meaningful decisions that will totally change your life for the better.

Face It; Don't Avoid It

There are three types of trauma: acute trauma, which is a result of a single incident; chronic trauma, which is repeated and prolonged, such as domestic violence or abuse; and complex trauma, which is exposure to varied and multiple traumatic events, often of an invasive interpersonal nature. Our bodies are conditioned to react whenever we encounter something that threatens our peace, or something that infringes on our values or property. It is one thing when you react and are free from the violator, but it is another when you are trapped in a cycle where the offender has taken your mind captive without your permission, and then hijacks and violates your body, consistently inflicting blows, and you are left defenseless, like a highway roadkill. It is easy to fall into depression and self-denial, and this creates a barrier by separating your mind from your present reality. It makes you numb to the constant pain, and you foolishly believe that your body belongs to them, and they can do whatever they want whenever they please.

This echoes from the bottom of my belly: the cries of my childhood. I was a child that was afraid of everything, even my own shadow—a lost child that felt she must have done something to deserve the bad things that happened.

We must face our past, stare it in the face, and sing the song of victory: "I am no longer a slave to fear." You have overcome so many darts that were meant to silence you, disable you, or even kill you. Let your life be a living testimony of the goodness of God—it is not luck. Facing your fears is one of the best ways to conquer them. Develop ways to overcome them one step at a time. If you fail to embark on this journey, you will develop a pattern of avoiding situations, places, or people that remind you of your past, and eventually this will unfortunately form a paralyzing pattern of behavior that would leave you emotionally bankrupt. It is human nature to avoid emotions that scare us; no one wants to walk into something that is painful—but how would you ever discover your strength if you were never tested? When we were going to school, the teacher would provide a test to all the students to gain an understanding of their knowledge. In life, we are given lessons based on our experiences, and are tested through our actions.

Don't avoid your fear; don't suppress it—if you do, then you will become a hostage of fear. You may think that hiding it would cause you less stress and pain. But in reality, what you are actually doing is denying yourself the opportunity that can lead to personal growth, peace, and joy. Instead of avoiding, accept your feelings of loss, and give yourself time to heal and to mourn any losses you've experienced. Time is the healer of all wounds. Don't force the healing process; rejoice over small victories. Don't see fear as a bad thing but rather an opportunity to expose yourself to that which you fear. Only then will you overcome it. Finally, visualize your life without fear—what are some of the things you need to do to make this a reality? Remember that the first step is to work on getting rid of toxic thoughts, since everything starts in the mind. Don't avoid facing your fears; face them. Applaud yourself for taking the steps necessary to conquer the inner enemy and command your outer existence to move to the rhythm of your new song. Nelson Mandela wrote: *"I learned that courage was not the absence of fear, but the triumph over it. The brave man is not he who does not feel afraid, but he who conquers that fear."* The presence of fear is an opportunity to build our character and create ways for us to find our way through it.

Chapter 3

Practice Gratitude and Contentment

Having experienced trauma myself, I know how difficult it is to laugh again, and to pick up the broken pieces of what is left of your life when you are crumbling inside. It is an exhausting struggle not knowing what to do to feel better. Coping with destructive, repetitive thoughts, and making it through another hour or minute, never mind getting through an entire day, can be almost impossible to handle. Unfortunately, this is the reality of many people who are processing, dealing with, and healing from a traumatic event. Trauma causes fear, but gratitude is the pathway to happiness. Gratitude helps to decrease fear by shifting your focus away from your anxiety, and instead providing solutions. Because our experiences, whether good or bad, form patterns that are then filtered in the brain, the end result is our attitudes. There is no denying that gratitude changes the brain. It has been found that feelings of gratitude directly activate brain regions associated with the neurotransmitter *dopamine*. Dopamine is that "feel good" neurotransmitter. It is important in the initiation of action, which means that with increased dopamine, you are more likely to have an improved mood, and feelings of reward and motivation. The key is to turn negative emotions into positive ones. In addition, gratitude plays an integral part in boosting your immune system.

Gratitude and contentment are a winning combination that reminds us to stay in the present, and therefore being mindful of everything around us. It is an intentional effort to evaluate every moment to count our blessings, no matter how small. The secret to a lifetime of happiness lies within us, but sometimes it is easy to take things for granted when you are dealing with overwhelming feelings of depression. The first thing we should do to seek contentment is to take stock of our situation and express gratitude. Being thankful for the things you have can put you in the headspace of knowing that things aren't nearly as bad as you sometimes make them out to be. It can give you the realization that, although things could be better, they are manageable for the time being. Contentment comes from within, rather than from external conditions. It depends on your attitude and how you see and respond to things. Even some people in severe circumstances can experience feelings of contentment.

Pay keen attention to your thoughts and things around you, but most importantly, to your interactions with others. The use of gratitude helps to unshackle the mind from toxic thoughts and negative emotions. So, if you are feeling stuck, overwhelmed, depressed, and fearful, it simply means that you have not activated the gratitude and contentment principle. When I was recovering from trauma, it was extremely hard to be grateful. I used to wonder what there was to be grateful about. I was stuck in this state for a long time, and I realized that my health was getting worse. I was in and out of the hospital, lost my hair, and was looking like a shadow of my former self. It was not until I introduced the gratitude principle that my life changed for the better. I started writing a few sentences about what contentment and gratitude feels like to me, as well as how to know when I am experiencing contentment. This worked for me because it put everything into perspective by shifting my attention away from toxic emotions, such as resentment and envy. In addition, I was able to introduce other people in my writing, who had helped me on my journey, and for whom I am blessed to have in my life. It became considerably harder for me to ruminate my negative experiences. When you practice gratitude, it starts a virtuous cycle in your mind that influences how you think and see the world. You focus on the positives in your life, and then you notice that there are more positives than previously realized.

You become more grateful for these and see more for which you have appreciation. Further, when you practice gratitude, your brain also releases hormones that encourage this cycle to continue. Steve Maraboli said, *"Sometimes life knocks you on your ass...get up, get up!!! Happiness is not the absence of problems; it's the ability to deal with them."*

Look at the Bigger Picture

The journey of a thousand miles starts with one step. There is a bigger picture of our lives than what we are seeing with our limited vision. A few years ago, I started the journey of obtaining my Canadian driver's licence, and I was once again introduced to the rear view mirror and windshield principle. There's a reason that the windshield is bigger than the rear view mirror: Where you're going is much more important than where you are. It is not the magnitude of what is happening in your life that matters, but rather your ability to look at the life that lies ahead, instead of allowing a fleeting moment to have dominance over your life. This is a helpful life metaphor, about driving a car: When you learn the basics of driving, you gain the habit of glancing back in the rear view to orient yourself. Occasionally looking back is important; however, you need to look ahead to get to your destination. It is easy to look back in regret, and feel stuck in what seems like an inescapable sense of self-blame. Life is a mirror—we can take occasional glances backwards; however, we must strive to look forward to viewing the ever-expanding horizon that lies ahead.

We have a limited vision of our lives, but instead of looking at the bigger picture, one should focus on seeing the complete picture of life. Think of what you are doing right now and what is important in your life, and imagine a life without this. Only then can you feel the importance of life, along with the correct prioritization of people, tasks, etc. When you can see the bigger picture and realize what is actually going on, you will quietly and calmly become the master of your own life. Your thoughts, feelings, and behaviors will carefully calibrate themselves with clarity, peace, understanding, and truth, in order to define a happy life. Our perceptions of life, and of others, differs in many ways; we can be looking at the same picture, yet it can have different meanings. On our journeys through life, we must prepare ourselves for many distractions that may threaten to throw us off course, but we need to stay focused. When you understand why certain people and circumstances are in your life, causing you joy or pain, you can cooperate with your soul's evolution. Many of us are wounded souls and continue the vicious cycle of hurting others, until we heal the wounds of our past that cause infection in our subconscious and keeps us from total fulfillment. We can also create opportunities to expand qualities that raise our consciousness.

The rear view mirror, even if it is small, is an important part of a vehicle. It aids the driver during overtaking, parking, driving in reverse, etc. The only time you should look at your past is to use it to measure your progress and motivation, but not do so with self-pity or shame.

You will feel worthy of receiving the abundant results that will inevitably come into your life. Much of self-concept and self-esteem begins with self-image. We experience ourselves as we see ourselves. Remain hopeful about the future, overcome your setbacks, maneuver the roadblocks, and forge the way forward, with a mind that is focused on the destination. Hope is not easily defined, but is impossible to embrace without faith. The more we search for meaning in what seems hopeless, the more we realize that our "hopelessness" is a state of mind, not a reality. Do something every single day to bring you closer to making your big picture a reality.

Protect Your Energy

Some people are emotional sponges: They soak up the problems of those around them. The lack of awareness of what is robbing our emotional energy, is a choice that only we can make; however, if we fail to pay attention to this, we are living carelessly. We absorb energy from other people, places, and different environments. By becoming more aware of the things and settings that change your energy, you will be able to protect it better. Pay attention to your mood—specifically with places, people, or situations that trigger a negative, even if very subtle, energy shift. Who and what changes your energy? Do certain interactions leave you feeling emotionally exhausted? Do you find yourself saying "yes" to things you don't feel like doing, just because you want to be polite or feel obligated to do them? Do you shrink your standards or your talents to please others? Once you have raised your standard of awareness, and have learned how to protect your energy, you are in a better headspace to discern what is allowed in your personal space.

We need to learn how to detach ourselves from other people's emotions, and not allow ourselves to be treated like an emotional dumping ground. Negative thought patterns can be fed for decades, especially when connected to a traumatic experience. This is created by negative experiences and expectations. The more energy you give them, the more energy they require, and the stronger their influence on your state of balance. I am sure most of us can testify to the fact that sometimes we can be in a good mood, and someone's opinions or expectations can change our perspectives. When someone says something negative, it can get stuck in your mind and play out over and over, undetected until you start to pay attention to it. Thoughts that are created out of fear, grief, blame, or anger can remain attached to your energy and cause you to attach the very thing you don't want. To clear this pattern, look at your life and see if you are attracting situations you don't like. If you are, you are somehow vibrating in alignment with them without your conscious awareness.

Since so many things demand our time and attention, we need to find ways to recharge and refocus our energy. When we find ways to connect to the things that replenish our energy, we consciously raise our awareness of things around us, and this makes it hard for us to fall victim to others. This century has seen its share of turmoil, pain, violence, etc. We are focused and glued to our television sets like white on rice. We are caught up in every headline happening around the world. Yet we have failed to deal with the things that are killing us slowing. The inner self is dying slowly every day; we have conquered outer space but are afraid of ourselves. Never think that you are "less than" because of your scarred past. Work on finding solutions instead of focusing on the problems. Everything that is happening in your life right now may not be a direct result of your own decisions, but it can be the decisions of others. When we are not mindful in having the ability to decipher the 5 Ws of our lives, we are unknowingly agreeing to have negative factors take dominance in our lives. A person's energy can tell you more about them than words; pay close attention.

> *"You draw to you the people and events which resonate*
> *with the energy that you are radiating.*
> *You attract what you are, so be the best."*
> *– Lynda Field*

Attract Good Karma

When we think of the word "karma," we tend to focus on the negative aspect of it and see it as retribution for something someone did to us. It simply means the word or deed of someone, which influences the future of that individual. But there is also "good karma," which is the good intent or good deed that contributes to a happier life. Attracting good karma is not hard; in fact, it is one of the easiest things we can do since it starts with us—yes, we are the architects of what we attract. We can start by first loving and forgiving ourselves for past wrongs. Most people, at one time or another, find themselves battling low self-esteem, self-blame, and self-doubt. We love others and would give anything to make them happy, yet we hate ourselves. It took me a long time to accept this. I called myself the worst names, and guess what? I was only digging a hole for myself. We can only attract good karma when we work on ourselves to eliminate toxic thoughts and emotions. Hold no grudges against anyone. This would only cause your growth to become stagnant, and would dim the light that would illuminate your future.

Practice Gratitude and Contentment

It took me a while to appreciate myself and become my own best friend, and I am still learning; but believe me, I have come a long way. I am now dating myself—yes, you heard me right—I take myself out on dates to the movies, to the gym, and to social events. I have also made peace with my past, and the universe is listening and taking notes. My story made the front headline of the newspaper in my country. I remember purchasing a newspaper and seeing my life flashing before me—it was an out-of-body experience. But I always knew that God was going to use my story to not only help others but to elevate me to a higher level. It is amazing that God can take your experience and make it your platform—like Joseph who was sold to slavery. The more painful your past, the higher you can soar in God's eyes. Never underestimate God and his reason for allowing pain and suffering; it is not without a greater purpose.

Practicing kindness and compassion is one of the easiest ways to send good karma into the world. The more we practice good karma, the less we attract bad karma. Sometimes we are quick to condemn others for the wrong they did to us, and sometimes we reply that their karma is coming, and we see it as something bad that is going to happen to that individual. What we fail to realize is that what that person did to us was a result of what we attracted; you need to work on yourself so that others can treat you the right way. I am not saying that people will always treat you well all the time, but when we are mindful of the energies we send out, we are laying the foundation for good karma to locate us. We can also allow the good karma to flow by, weeding out the bad seeds that had been planted years ago, and have now become gigantic trees. Spend time in quiet introspection, and see this as a time for doing deep soul searching as you explore your personal role in all that has transpired in your life. Embark on this with an open mind and without being judgemental of yourself, since this might unveil some things about the real you, and why you are responsible for some of the things that are happening in your life. The purpose is to gain understanding, not to place blame.

Intentional efforts and actions, repeated over a period of time, can reap good karma. Maharishi Mahesh Yogi said, *"Problems or suc-*

cesses, they all are the results of our own actions. The philosophy of action is that no one else is the giver of peace or happiness. One's own karma, one's own actions are responsible to come to bring either happiness or success." Make it your mission to attract things into your life that will attract good karma. We can change the tapestry of our thinking, about the way we view our past circumstances, by staying alert in regard to the things we attract. Sometimes we are not even aware of some of the things we allow to take lodgement for long periods of time in our minds. Start guarding your mind today, because it is the gateway to your soul and, ultimately, will become the prerequisite to either life's successes or failures.

Celebrate You

Sometimes we wait on the big things to happen in our lives before we can celebrate, but every day we are above the ground is enough reason to celebrate. Small efforts deserve to be acknowledged. I live with this motto every day: "Once there is life, there is hope." Hope is the fuel that lights the way in this dark world. Life is to be lived and celebrated, but most of us are just existing; we are not really living. So, what is the difference? When we fail to live up to our full potential, we allow fear and our past to dictate the future. The sad reality is that we can't celebrate because we are yet to find out who we are, and what the purpose is for our existence. We live our lives in a bubble, afraid to be seen or heard. We feel it is okay to hide how great we truly are, because we are afraid that others might think we are proud or boastful. My sisters/brothers, you are destined for greatness. God never made a mistake when he molded you into the unique person that you are today. Don't allow circumstances from your past to blur your vision, and don't ever for a minute believe the negative voices that tell you that you can't be great.

Recovering from a trauma may have taken its toll on your ability to love and appreciate who you are. But this is also something to celebrate: You are still alive; you survived it all. There is a reason God kept you, so don't waste another minute in emotional bondage. You are the one in control of your emotions, and you are the one making decisions every day that can either motivate or hinder your future. In today's society, we tend to gravitate toward things and occasions that make us feel good. We celebrate birthdays, anniversaries, our pets' birthdays, and even when finding $10.00 that we lost, in the pocket of our favorite blue jeans. Yet we neglect the most important celebration: "YOU." When we find time to celebrate the small things, we open the door for positivity to flow into our lives. When was the last time you took some time from your busy schedule to pamper yourself?

As a child, I can recall my grandmother purchasing expensive dinnerware, and then putting it away all year; but every Christmas holiday, she would take it out, wash it, and then put it away again. She would repeat this every year, with absolutely no desire of using it. From that experience, I have learned to never put away my most precious prized possessions—life is short and should be lived in the present. My family is fascinated with the way I celebrate life. I will frequently purchase champagne and pop the cork spontaneously. Everyone has something to celebrate; it's just that some people are so burdened by life that they fail to see the beauty of life. Dare to do something different every day. Routine can be boring, and it keeps us in our comfort zone. Humans are creatures of comfort. Our comfort zone is our natural, neutral state and place where stress is minimal, and where we know what's coming next and can plan accordingly. If we are stuck in familiarity, security, and certainty—the "comfort zone"—it will blind us to seeing reasons to celebrate and to challenge ourselves by doing something new.

It all boils down to our attitude, which can cloud our perception of things around us. Take the time to enjoy the sunset or smell the roses. I can't emphasize enough how short life is; treasure the time you have on the earth, and make every second count. Take the time to celebrate and to appreciate yourself; stop putting off the things you dream of doing, and pursue them NOW.

*"Learn to get in touch with the silence within yourself,
and know that everything in life has a purpose.
There are no mistakes, no coincidences; all events
are blessings given to us to learn from."*
– Elisabeth Kubler-Ross

There Is Beauty in Silence

The world is constantly changing, and human nature is constantly gravitating toward the latest gadgets. There is no denying that technology is pervasive throughout our lives. It has affected the way we communicate; it is a constant presence in our relationships, and has impacted the way we interact with those closest to us. Silence in itself has extreme strength, yet we ignore its importance. In silence, we can learn a lot about ourselves and those around us. The problem is that most of us are afraid of silence because we are afraid of dealing with our inner most thoughts. We are easily distracted and are hooked up to apps that offer unprecedented exposure to the innermost thoughts and actions of others, but in spite of the world creating different types of mediums for interactions, we are still socially deprived. Silence is a source of great strength. There is beauty in silence, and in the things that can never be replaced and are essential to our total being. We are socially deprived because we have lost the meaning of communication.

Silence can teach us to be satisfied with what we have, no matter how small. Perhaps it would be wiser to talk less, since volume speaks louder than words. By immersing ourselves in moments of silence, we can collect our thoughts and take a break from the noise. When our minds are quiet, we can think deeply, and our inner voices are able to speak to us. It's only in these precious moments that we experience our own divinity. There is a lot to learn from being still and quiet. Many of us don't like to be alone, let alone be silent. Being left with our own thoughts can seem daunting. Sometimes we want to keep ourselves busy so that we don't have deal with our inner emotions. By trusting the silence, you realise that you have the freedom to dictate your thoughts. You are in control of how you think and feel. Let go and trust the silence. This has taught me the importance of shaping my thinking. Take time each day to notice your thoughts, and let go of thoughts and emotions that are bad for you.

Silence is a healer; it allows us to gain clarity and introspection of our thoughts, which can lead to solving conflicts and releasing tension from the body and mind. We also gain trust in silence because it plays an integral role in highlighting our inner strength; and like a magnet, we can eliminate negative emotions by building positive ones, thus making us more emotionally resilient. We are quick to fix our outer selves, but our outer selves are slowing dying from neglect and lack of emotional balance. Humanity has traveled great distances to conquer outer space, but we are yet to conquer our inner space. In addition, when we are in tune with the universe, we are nurturing our inner selves; our characters change when we listen more and talk less. We understand that words are feeble when they don't feed the mind or nurture our souls.

We need to listen to what the universe is trying to say to us, and we can't accomplish this if we are busy and distracted with temporal things that only subtract instead of add to our personal growth and well-being. Furthermore, we fail to realise the wisdom that we can accumulate by simply spending time cleansing our thoughts daily. We are on a quest for external things, and we keep accumulating more and more, like a human vacuum, but the most important part of us, we fail to nurture. Silence forces us to confront the real enemy: ourselves. Find a balance in your life, and embark on a mission to invest more in your personal life. More importantly, guard your space and schedule a private time to nourish your inner being. If we fail to do this, we are robbing ourselves of living up to our full potential. It is more important than anything you do, because it's from there that you'll find the strength, purpose, and self-composure to be a better person to yourself and others.

Escaping Ugly

*"Silence is the great teacher, and to learn its lessons,
you must pay attention to it. There is absolutely no substitute
for the creative inspiration, knowledge, and the stability that comes
from knowing how to contact your core of inner silence."*
– Deepak Chopra

Chapter 4

Accessing Resources, Internal or External

Recovering from trauma is a long process and will stay with you for a lifetime. It is vital to embark on a journey of healing. Brainstorming various avenues and resources is key. Accessing resources can be quite a daunting experience, but with the right resources and social support, it becomes easier to cope. Accessing resources should be something that needs to be implemented early on in your experience, to help in balancing your emotions. For many who are navigating the waters of a traumatic experience, it takes utilizing both external and internal resources. Once those resources begin to be activated, many will move toward healing and strength. It is imperative to remember that you are not alone in your experience. Resources help in your understanding, and with the addition of the support of others, you become stronger. Everyone can develop different ways of coping. Whether it is accessing internal resources or developing coping skills, it is necessary to identify what works best for you. However, in the final analysis, accessing external resources can help to add balance to your life and assist in improving internal resources.

People in general are resourceful, but pain can cloud our vision, and our bodies are always looking for ways to cope and find relief from the symptoms of trauma. When people learn to turn those efforts toward positive coping skills and strengths, the journey of recovery goes to a new level. Reclaiming your strength after trauma is a perfect ingredient, which will play an integral part in your recovery. After a traumatic event, many people will emerge with new strengths, more resources, and new skills that will help them to be more resilient. Furthermore, with the right resources from a professional, they may be able to identify strengths within themselves that they were not aware of.

Due to the prevalence of abuse, violence, and turmoil, which can then cause trauma, many organizations and services have introduced trauma-informed care in their practices. This simply means an organizational structure and treatment that involves understanding, recognizing, and responding to any types of trauma. It emphasizes psychological and emotional safety for both consumers and providers, and helps survivors rebuild a sense of control and empowerment. Abuse, whether physical, emotional, verbal, or sexual, can have long-term effects on your mental health. People who have gone through any form of trauma have a higher risk of developing a mental health condition, such as depression, anxiety, or post-traumatic stress disorder (PTSD). Accessing internal resources can help with your ability to cope, and it can also become an excellent healing mechanism.

It is important to note that when you are on the road to recovery, you may encounter something similar to withdrawal symptoms, which can include depression, anxiety, nausea, or insomnia. You may experience difficult and volatile emotions, but it is just your body and mind trying to cope. Allow yourself to feel whatever you are feeling, without judgement or guilt, and to be patient with the pace of the healing process, knowing that time is the healer of all wounds.

> *"Our wounds are often the openings into the best and most beautiful part of us."*
> – David Richo

It is only in adversity that we can truly discover our strengths. Just like the potter molding a broken vessel, we are made truly whole when we discover the best kept secret: to truly know who we are. Recovery allows us to find deeper meaning to the WHY of our existence. Our internal forces become greater than our external realities.

Rewrite Your Story

The ugliness of trauma may have been your worse experience, but the beauty is that you can change your story by writing a new one. You can create a story out of your ordeal. You may have unconsciously developed negative opinions about yourself, but when you rewrite your story, you are doing so with new perspectives, and thus the result would be different. The initial story of your trauma is an outdated version, and thus there is a need to write a revised version. The new chapter would tell the story of how a victim was able to become an overcomer. For many years, I felt like my story was too ugly to share. I would frequently have out-of-body experiences, where I would be in denial of my role as the victim in my story. It was not until I took full ownership of my experience that I was able to see the beauty of my experience. My story is beautiful and unique, and I am happy that I was fortunate enough to be chosen for this, because the latest version of my story is greater than my past.

A few years ago, I was a participant at a women's event, and the keynote speaker was a pastor from New York. When I shared my story, many women broke down in tears; some had anxiety attacks, and emergency personnel even had to be summoned to the location. Many have built walls to separate their bad experiences from who they truly are. Suppressed pain can eventually cause an eruption that can threaten your present peace. I can recall one attendee that mentioned she had been hiding her trauma for many years, and after hearing my story, she was motivated to work on becoming more transparent. In addition, she felt a sense of relief that she was now motivated to become an advocate for change. Your story can appear too painful to explain, much less put into words. One simple technique that worked for me was to start by writing short poems. This was helpful in lessening the pain, and created a more simple way of healing. In addition, once again, writing is a technique that can help the mind to find emotional balance.

Telling your story allows you to finally muster the courage to tell the truth to yourself before you can tell it to others. Your existence was once based on falsehood—you once believed what others thought of you—and unfortunately your own environment was a product of this betrayal. Retelling your story gives you a chance to be the captain of your ship. Be an ambassador for others. Not many people understand how trauma affects an individual, unless you are talking from the perspective of a survivor. Allow your story to motivate others to know that they are not alone, and use your story as a motivational tool. When you suffer a traumatic event, it can be painful to revisit the pain, but in order to heal, you must first be open to yourself. A closed wound can't fully heal until you expose it to the elements that were meant to break it in the first place. As a child growing up in the Caribbean, I can recall many people having a "sore foot" that would take forever to heal. If not treated properly, it could lead to more complicated and complex medical issues. The reason for this is, if a sore is covered, it would take longer to heal. We have to first accept past pain and hurt before there is healing. Trauma memories will revisit us more often if we surpass it—the more you push it away, the more it will appear.

Some aspects of my experience with trauma, I still can't remember. I have tried on many occasions but to no avail. Keeping your trauma a secret re-enforces feelings of shamefulness, since you may think that others would be judgmental if you were to share your story. Feelings of empowerment come when you accept your story and embrace your painful past, while creating the opportunity to rewrite a better version of your story.

Practice Self-Sufficiency

Self-esteem is a major part of the recovery process after trauma, since it can become fragile unless you implement self-sufficiency. To be self-sufficient is the quality of feeling secure and content with oneself, and having a deep-rooted sense of inner completeness and stability. It is a means of recovering your self-esteem; however, this is just a part of it. The aim is to establish a feeling of wholeness and stability in your life, and self-esteem is one of the ingredients that can aid you on the road to recovery. People with strong self-sufficiency are not concerned about the opinions of others. They have a deep-rooted sense of their own self-worth. They have built a strong internal force that makes them more resilient to tragedies. Years of experience has taught them to safeguard their sense of independence, and to protect their self-worth. Self-sufficient people are authentic. They are firm believers in the concept of "what you see is what you get," which means that they strive to always exhibit honesty and transparency.

Part of trauma is feeling powerless. To feel empowered is to reclaim your power. You can accomplish this by monitoring your actions to conquer fear and uncertainty. Self-sufficiency helps in regulating your emotions and can be a key factor in building your sense of independence. The liberation from bondage is a journey of establishing your independence. Many trauma survivors are bombarded with a flood of many emotions, which can create confusion in the mind. It is necessary to find a balance and look within yourself to find help. In building survival skills, and building self-sufficiency, you need to disregard asking others for permission when you have it within you. When we bring others into our experience, we are opening ourselves to negative feedback, which can derail our self-esteem. The criticism of others can cause us to lose focus, and decreases our ability to nurture self-sufficiency. This is not to say that you can't confide in others or solicit the opinions of others; what it means is to exercise the power within you to make your own decisions with confidence before you ask others.

Make a decision to educate yourself on trauma. Many times we are afraid of exploring issues of trauma. But it is necessary to learn more about the subject of trauma and how it impacts your mental health. We can't control everything, but we can work daily on building healthy and emotional self-sufficiency. The work of building your mental health is a part of building self-esteem and self-sufficiency. Since many survivors of trauma may not readily access professional help right away, it is necessary to adopt some fundamental attributes inwardly that would become building blocks for your success. Finally, another important part of building self-esteem is spiritual self-sufficiency. In building spiritual self-sufficiency, you can gain the skills/knowledge that you need to be mentally and emotionally prepared for any type of disaster or turmoil. A solid and healthy relationship with God is an integral part of building spiritual self-control.

> *"The amount of satisfaction you get from life depends*
> *largely on your own ingenuity, self-sufficiency,*
> *and resourcefulness. People who wait around for life*
> *to supply their satisfaction usually find boredom instead."*
> – William C. Menninger

Be Your Own Hero

For most individuals, if you asked the question, "Who is a hero? the natural reaction is to look at someone outside of themselves. We take on the mindset of what is portrayed on TV or social media; we look at images of Superman, Hulk, or Captain America. But in the modern-day life version, it can be anyone who exemplifies exceptional qualities, or who exhibit resiliency in spite of adverse circumstances. Everyone has a hero living inside; we just need to accept responsibility for our own future. Too many times, we go through life and accept whatever is given to us, without question. We allow people to mistreat us, and we seldom voice our concerns, because we are afraid of "mashing anyone's corn." The most important lesson trauma has taught me is to fear only GOD. I have adopted a lack of tolerance for mediocracy and negativity. I have suffered for too long and was without a voice. Becoming my own advocate and speaking up for the most disenfranchised in society, has become one of my best qualities. When you encounter the darkest pit of an experience, you are driven, like Joseph in the Bible, to create beauty from ashes.

The hero's journey is not an easy one; you must make the decision to stay on course, weather the storms of life, and stay on the path until the end. A hero is not someone who starts something and never sees it to fruition. They have built a reputation where nothing but greatness resides. Most importantly, a hero is self-made. They are not broken easily, because their dependence is not on others but on their inner strength. They have learned and implement qualities of a hero—for example, being a positive role model, serving others, inspiring others, and taking action to challenge themselves. The most vital part of a hero is their ability to grow through intense adversity and turmoil. Remember in the movies how Superman wore regular clothes through the day, and was transformed once he put on his cape. We are transformed when we ignore the external critics and tap into the inner source. When we do, the obstacles that seem so indestructible will crumble.

Survivors of trauma experience a high degree of hopelessness, which can blind one to their present reality since it dims their level of awareness. Without "HOPE," we are like the "living dead" on Earth. We are neither alive nor dead; our existence is limited to a lukewarm state. Hope is what ignites awareness and creates the fuel that moves us from the attitude of surviving to thriving. Heroes are busy people that are motivated to be winners, regardless of the odds that are stacked against them. I truly believe that the greatest gift one can give oneself is the ability to celebrate small victories every day. I mentioned in an earlier chapter, my practice of keeping a bottle of champagne in my home. I am always popping bottles for what others would consider small things. If I have learned anything during this century, it is the fragility and uncertainty of life. Enjoy it while you still have life and teeth left, and make the most of every second of the day. Living a life of regret is one stress that you need to avoid in your latter years.

Heroes are made through adversity. Many people underestimate the ability of a modern-day hero, since many may appear like the underdog and are often overlooked as lacking outer strength. In the movies, a hero emerges when the innocent are in peril—they are motivated to act on behalf of others.

> *"Today is a new day! You have the opportunity to pick up life's pen and change your story. Become the hero; the greatest hero in your story, and you'll see how excited your life will be. You will watch your goals and dreams transition from something you simply hoped for, to something within your powerful grasp."*
> – Dr. Steve Maraboli

Implementing Self-Care

After trauma, self-care can take many forms. It all depends on the individual and what works best for them. The most important thing is to start small—maybe taking a break for a few minutes per day—and then expand with deeper, more meaningful techniques as time goes on. I became aware of a deep understanding of self-care when I completed my studies as a social worker. Before this, my understanding was very vague. I thought it was selfish to practice self-care. Many individuals are confronted daily with triggers, flashbacks, and emotional imbalance, but by implementing self-care, one can see improvement in their daily lives. When trying to find your sense of self and reclaiming your power, it can't be done without spending quality time in self-care. Self-care is divided into many parts, which can include physical self-care, spiritual, emotional, mental, etc. After trauma, the body goes through a "reprogram" stage, where one must work daily on getting rid of toxic thought patterns. Since self is the paramount figure in this picture, it is imperative to focus on healing and restoration around "SELF." The caring of yourself helps to bring focus to pertinent issues that affect your well-being and things that can work collaboratively to strengthen your resiliency from outer attacks.

The process of self-care is very broad and can include a variety of techniques that can be educational and fun. We can learn so much from ourselves and those around us if only we could get rid of all the tension that forms a regular part of our lives. Self-care helps to declutter our mental closets by getting rid of old habits, toxic thoughts, and emotional baggage. We can't be truly free if we are still operating on the old version of ourselves. It simply means that we are the biggest fools to believe that we can do the same thing, year in and year out, and expect different results. One of the best ways to make sure you're giving your body and mind what it needs to heal, is to check in with yourself. Take note of what you've done and haven't done daily; think about what you want to do. What will help you feel better, or more at ease with yourself?

Self-care allows you to put yourself first. I should once again emphasize that "it is not selfish to indulge yourself in self-care." In fact, it is the best gift you can give yourself. However, do everything in moderation. Self-care doesn't have to be expensive. It is the simple and less costly things in life that can be the most effective. For example, maintaining a healthy diet, getting 8 hours of sleep every night, or practicing grounding techniques. These can do wonders to help regulate your emotions, build a healthy immune system, and bring you in touch with your environment. Trauma acts as a catalyst for us to learn how to better engage in self-care, and introduces us to endless modalities for healing and expressing ourselves, which enables us to channel our crisis into transformation.

During the early stage of my self-care journey, I was fortunate to connect with other survivors, and it was through accessing and forging links with these communities that I found the most healing. My biggest problem at this time was self-sabotaging thoughts. Learning the method of reversing these thoughts, by replacing them with positive self-affirmation, was a sweet victory that I was pleased to celebrate.

Escaping Ugly

The "self" is dying a slow death every second of the day,
and if we fail to rescue ourselves,
then what use are we to humanity?"
— Deloris Gardner

Our minds are storehouses for intense emotions of grief, rage, and past hurt, and the intensity increases in the aftermath of abuse and trauma. In order to combat feelings of numbness and rage, we need to protect ourselves, and we can start by filtering our energy into the care of "self" before anything else.

Building Social Capital

Maintaining interactions with others, and implementing new contacts, can help to enlarge your social circle. Since many survivors of trauma suffer from isolation, loneliness, and guilt, connecting with others and building their social circle plays a key role in their lives. A good way of building social capital is through volunteering, attending workshops, and daily interactions with others. You need to forge relationships that would be beneficial for you when you need it. It is developed through investment, which gives us a sense of belonging. It is a space where people are working as team players, and feelings are reciprocated. A strong network is more than money in the bank, which can serve as an asset. It helps by protecting our mental health and aiding in alleviating some of the pressure of day-to-day living. Many individuals are living in communities with absolutely no knowledge of relevant resources. Building your social capital in collaboration with community partners takes trust, reciprocity, collective action, and participation.

Social capital is an individual commodity that is developed through the partnership and shared experiences of those we interact with. In rebuilding your life after trauma, expanding your social circle would play an integral part of the recovery process. Trauma, by nature,

Accessing Resources, Internal or External

thrives on isolation. When you connect with people—family, friends, colleagues, and acquaintances—you are tapping into humanity and discovering your role in the universe. The result of trauma is a broken soul, a disoriented mind, and a discouraged spirit. When you network with others, it helps to add some level of completeness; when someone in your network is down, you can lift that someone up. A very vital part of rebuilding life after trauma, and finding your place in the world, is to work on reconnecting your soul to humanity.

Don't allow shame or discouragement to be a barrier to building your social life. When you connect with others with similar experiences, you will come to the realization that you are not alone. You will build a comradery of individuals from diverse backgrounds. We have the tendency to dwell on the destruction of something for too long before we can refocus on creating a new canvas. Always be mindful that we are only given challenges that our Creator knows we can overcome. What you have gone through is not without a purpose, and it is not in vain—God will reveal it in time. Your life is under construction, and the next step is to get your tools and construction hat, because the only way forward after trauma is to rebuild.

"You are the sum total of the people you meet and interact with in the world. Whether it's your family, peers, or co-workers, the opportunities you have and the things that you learn all come through doors that other people open for you."
– Tanner Colby

We must be willing to work on transforming our pain into action. Before trauma, I was a big procrastinator and I lived a carefree life; I took many things for granted. Trauma is my motivation and has helped me to thrive every day to live a purpose-driven life. A life without purpose is not living but existing. Social capital not only helps to give us a fresh perspective on things that concern us, but widens the equation to include those that help in fostering our growth.

Notes

Chapter 5

Controlling Triggers

According to the dictionary, triggers are people, words, opinions, or any situations that provoke an intense and excessive emotional reaction within us. Common emotions that we experience while being triggered include anger, rage, sadness, and fear. Triggers frequently occur after a traumatic event and can be associated with post-traumatic stress disorder (PTSD). It is often a memory that reminds you of a traumatic event. It can be classified into two categories: internal and external triggers. Identifying your triggers can be upsetting and can potentially start a flashback, but it is necessary to know what they are by making a list of them. I was constantly haunted by my past and would experience extreme flashbacks, which eventually led to many anxiety attacks. A trigger can occur at any time or place; it plays on your senses, which can be smelling, hearing, seeing, tasting, or feeling. It is like experiencing an emotional roller coaster ride, and this can resurface at any time, without warning. That is why it is necessary to identify what your triggers are, and to work on ways of not only coping but thriving.

Managing your emotions can be one of your greatest assets; however, it takes a lot of practice. Whenever you experience positive feelings, make sure you take time to slow down and notice the pleasant experiences. Savor the goodness, joy, and comfort; then reflect on one thing each day that makes you feel good. By paying attention to what emotions are working in your favor, it would build your awareness level. In addition, this would help to build your resilience while increasing your ability to experience more good emotions. Life becomes more worthwhile when we learn to make small changes in our lives every day. The great news is that triggers are something that can be controlled with practice, and you can start by creating positive experiences that will lead to positive memories. Emotions help us to communicate with others.

Lifestyle is associated with triggers, so in order to balance your emotions, it is imperative to change old habits and activities to new ones. Take small steps gradually, to expand your window of tolerance. Avoiding or staying away from things that trigger you may work in the moment, but it might not work in the long run. Start small and work your way up. Continue until you have successfully managed your emotions to the point that the experience is no longer a trigger. Confront your trigger by briefly going to the places where you are triggered, and then leave. Based on your reaction, acknowledge your feelings and work on overcoming the causes of the trigger.

Change your perception of yourself: Instead of looking at yourself as a victim, think of yourself as a powerful force that would remove the veil of self-deception. Be honest about yourself and your feelings, because anxiety can cause negative thoughts and delay the healing process.

"Highly sensitive people are too often perceived as weaklings or damaged goods. To feel intensely is not a symptom of weakness; it is the trademark of the truly alive and compassionate. It is not the empath who is broken; it is society that has become dysfunctional and emotionally disabled. There is no shame in expressing your authentic feelings. Those who are at times described as being a 'hot mess' or having 'too many issues,' are the very fabric of what keeps the dream alive for a more caring, humane world. Never be ashamed to let your tears shine a light in this world."
– Anthon St. Maarten

Emotional Intelligence

Many experts believe that emotional intelligence is more important than IQ, and is certainly a better predictor for success, quality of relationships, and overall success. I was always fascinated with the concept of emotional intelligence. All of humanity, regardless of race, class, or educational background, is coming up short on the emotional intelligence list. The reason for this can be the emphasis that is placed on educational intelligence, but little is placed on how to manage emotions. Many of us are emotional wrecks, who are clueless on how to control our emotions. Could this be the reason why we are facing so many issues in our world today, since there are many benefits that can be deprived from a healthy mind? Emotional intelligence is "being smart about your feelings." We need to develop an awareness of how our emotions drive our decisions and behaviors, which can then have an impact on how we influence others. As a survivor of any form of trauma, you are already starting from a place of intense pain, where one's emotions are out of whack.

In today's society, not many people talk about emotional intelligence, since some may consider it as a soft skill. It is a deep understanding of how to use your emotions and place a high emphasis on how you want others to see you. People with high levels of emotional intelligence are happier and more confident, and they thrive to make a positive impact on the world. Does emotional intelligence matter? It absolutely does. The way we interact with others is of paramount importance. In today's society, many people are emotionally bankrupted; they hide their emotions behind the latest emoji, and this has replaced their true feelings. Emotional intelligence is the gateway to a well-balanced life. When we fail to manage our emotions, we create avenues where the external forces take precedence over our lives.

A high emotional intelligence helps us to be stronger internal motivators, which can reduce procrastination, increase self-confidence, and improve our ability to focus on our goals. It also allows us to create better networks of support, handle setbacks, and preserve a more resilient outlook. Our ability to delay gratification and see the long term, directly affects our ability to succeed. In other words, living a successful and fulfilling life is closely related to your ability to be emotionally balanced. When we fail to pay attention to our emotions due to our busy lifestyles, or suppress them, things will eventually get worse. The more we try to put our emotions behind us, the more uncontrollable they become. Whenever we have an emotional reaction, it is because we have unresolved issues. In building emotional intelligence, you must get familiar with your emotions, and understand why you are experiencing certain feelings at any given time.

*"Emotional intelligence is a way of recognizing,
understanding, and choosing how we think, feel, and act.
It shapes our interactions with others, and our understanding
of ourselves. It defines how and what we learn;
it allows us to set priorities; it determines most of our actions.
Research suggests it is responsible for as much as
80 percent of the success in our lives."*
– J. Freedman

Challenge Yourself

The human body is the perfect metaphor for understanding the importance of change. We are consistently changing, evolving, and replenishing. The body is built to adapt and respond to the demands that are placed on it. It is the natural law of life. A major setback is that we tend to avoid the things in life that we deem difficult, and we are quick to move on to things that we classify as easy. It is human nature to resist change, but our comfort zone can never propel us to grow. Change is constant, and we can develop many long-lasting character traits through change. Challenges and problems are important parts of life that give you experiences, make you learn, and help you to become wiser and stronger. Problems make us grow, and they shape us. The biggest problem people have is that they hope for a life without problems. This is an impossible goal and would lead to a boring life without character. Trauma helps in shaping your experience, and it is indeed a difficult and painful road for many to travel. But we must be willing to embrace change in all its forms in order to experience complete healing.

Painful experiences will not disappear from our lives, so the sooner we are willing to embrace them, the more we can learn from them. An ordinary piece of coal must endure years of pressure to transform into a sparkling diamond, and to be a precious and valuable piece of jewelry. Challenges force us to form our consciousness and become more evolved and enlightened. Most people are of the notion that life should be a happy and smooth road all the time. So, when we are faced with difficult situations, we panic and lose our balance. What's important to understand is that all the pain we experience from difficult situations, is a direct result of our ability to process it in our internal world. We have the power to manage our reactions by making wise decisions and choosing thoughts that steer us toward calmer waters, just like a captain of a ship steers the ship away from storms or rough waters.

When we are confronted with unexpected storms, which may catch us by surprise, we should see it as a learning experience. The challenges are placed in your life to help you grow and to build your inner strength. Clearly, challenges need to be accepted as a part of life and our growth process. Ultimately, you will see that the universe is set up to facilitate the growth, evolution, and expansion of the consciousness of all living beings, including your own. Trauma may have caused discomfort in your experience, but you can't get rid of it with a magic wand.

Not only do challenges allow you to grow individually, but they also create opportunities to live life to your full potential. In addition, we gain awareness of various knowledge and skills that help shape our experience. Trauma may have placed a spoke in our wheel, but we have the power to learn those lessons and liberate ourselves from the bondage of self-sabotage. Once again, the faster we are willing to accept every challenge instead of seeing it negatively, the faster we can decide to accept it as an opportunity to grow and become better, not only for ourselves but for all humanity.

> *"The ultimate measure of a man is not where he stands in moments of comfort and convenience, but where he stands at times of challenges and controversy."*
> – Martin Luther King

Stop Procrastinating

We are all guilty of procrastinating at some point in our lives. Many people don't see procrastinating as a deterring factor that can eventually negatively alter their lives. Procrastination and time management work hand in hand, and since many individuals can become overwhelmed with many trauma related issues, it can affect their mental state and can lead to imbalance. People love to push things aside that they planned, due to work or just being lazy, and this can lead to a stressful life if not corrected. In addition, procrastinating can affect your self-esteem and cause you to be unproductive. People with low self-esteem often underestimate themselves and will not achieve their full potential, which causes a rise in the rate of failure. This causes an increase of fear of failure, and fear of not achieving perfection. Many do not realize it, but by accomplishing any given task on time, it builds confidence and can tremendously improve the way you embrace future tasks.

Everyone procrastinates at some point, but people have developed the tendency to avoid their obligations so often that it can result in a spiral of emotions, which can have a snowball effect. Because we can be quick to dismiss it as a minor problem, we overlook the fact that it has far-reaching effects, and more than we may even realize. The reason we may delay accomplishing a task, can be because of hidden fears that we are not ready to acknowledge, or it could be something that doesn't motivate us. There are many negative outcomes to bear in mind before you procrastinate, and these could cause you to reassess your decisions before you make them. A couple of examples are (A) loss of precious time, and (B) losing opportunities that you may never recover, and not being able to meet your goals. Procrastination is the killer of our precious time. To avoid bitterness and resentment of self, it is imperative to cultivate a life of living in the moment without regrets, and you can start by getting rid of procrastinating for good.

The worst part of procrastinating is waking up one day and realizing that you have wasted many years by being unproductive. This is a horrible state, and you may wish that you could turn back the hands of time, but nothing will ever change; so you must live with the feelings of regrets. Never put off until tomorrow what you can do today; we are not guaranteed anything in life but our present reality. Because of low self-esteem and the added weight of procrastination, it can cause a vicious cycle of further damage to your overall being. Furthermore, it can eat away at your self-confidence and can cause you to doubt your ability.

In trying to re-establish yourself after trauma, your reputation for keeping your word has a far-reaching effect on you as a person. Procrastination can inevitably tarnish your reputation, since people don't take empty promises too lightly. Besides damaging your reputation, you are also damaging your self-esteem and self-confidence. Many people don't think about the far-reaching effects of prolonged procrastination—the health implications are very damaging. Procrastination can be linked to many mental health issues, such as depression and anxiety.

> *"The best possible way to prepare for tomorrow is*
> *to concentrate with all your intelligence, all your enthusiasm,*
> *on doing today's work superbly today. That is the only possible*
> *way you can prepare for the future."*
> – Dale Carnegie

Contentment vs Complacency

Contentment and complacency are two words that are often confused and misused. There is a fundamental difference between the two. Being content means that you accept the reality of your situation without complaining or resenting it. When you are content, you work to change the things you can, and accept the things you can't. You do so without being disheartened. One can become comfortable wallowing in self-pity, and afraid to accept their present reality. Growth can only take place in the acceptance of one's past and finding solutions to eliminate any sign of stagnation. Complacency can cause a barrier in the healing process. There is a big danger in complacency, since it allows us to be in a state where we are comfortable with our present state, with no means of improving our lives. It can become highly contagious.

In a sense, after a traumatic experience, we let ourselves go, and it is natural that we may need a brief period to come to grips with what has happened. However, it is not okay to remain in that state for a long time, or to make excuses for our lack of growth or motivation. The longer we put up with mediocracy, the more unproductive we can become, and the more excuses we use to cover up our shortcomings. Complacency will eat away any potential for change to occur in our lives. It is something that we may consider to be a small issue; or sad to say, we may not even consider it to be a problem. You cannot deal with change effectively if you are complacent, because there is absolutely no avenue for change if you find yourself in this state. If you embark on the road of change, it can be a big shock to your system. Furthermore, complacency tends to foster complacent activities such as watching TV or playing video games, when that time could have been spent growing and improving your current state. Foster activities that promote growth and self-improvement.

Our time here on earth is very precious and limited, and it is imperative for all of us to embrace an attitude of urgency in order to live life to the fullest while being productive members of society. COVID-19 has completely changed my perspective of life and the need to live in the moment, while living the life God predestined for me. Many people are making investments into various ventures, yet they fail to invest in themselves. The attitude of complacency is like stashing your money under a mattress, and expecting it to grow or yield interest, only to have inflation eat it away. People put their investment into something that will yield some sort of interest, or would reap more than what they put in. You are the biggest investment to the world, and you can decide what value you place on your life, or decline in value due to bad decisions or habits.

So how is it possible for one's value to decline? When you are complacent, you tend to be unaware of the things that are going on around you, and you miss opportunities that are right in front your face. Bad habits, practiced over time, dull one's senses to things that diminish their self-worth and hinder their ability to be progressive in life. Complacency encourages the absolute minimum. We are afraid to rock the boat of safety; therefore, we remain in the sea of sameness—we are afraid to bring things into our lives that might upset the balance. Let us take the same approach as we do with our jobs: If we give the absolute minimum on the job, we might be on the chopping block. The prerequisite to this is to take the time to learn new skills and make improvements, since doing the bare minimum will not help in getting you a promotion.

Make Long/Short-Term Goals

"I am going to make this bold statement:
'A life without a sense of direction is pale
in comparison to a ship without a captain.'"
– Deloris Gardner

To date, most of what I was able to accomplish over the years is attributed to taking strategic steps in laying the foundation of well-planned goals, mixed with prayer and a burning desire to eliminate mediocracy. Failure is not a word in my vocabulary, and I refuse to use certain words: *like, if, but, rather, when*. When we understand how powerful words are, then we learn to be selective when we speak. Goal setting is a prerequisite for many successful stories. Nothing in life just happens, and nothing can ever fall into our laps without much effort. Just as oxygen is needed to keep us alive, so are goals important to propel our lives forward. These are the first steps one should take on the journey to a successful and productive life. It is one thing to set goals, but applying this knowledge is the key.

When we experience painful memories, goals help to keep us focused. They bring everything into perspective and refocus our energies on the important things in life. If we do not have a target, how would we know to shoot the arrow? Hitting the bullseye is not done without well-thought-out planning. "If we fail to plan, we are planning to fail." We tend to be suspicious of the negative things people say about us, yet we fail to recognize the self-sabotaging thoughts we feed our minds every day. Before you point a finger at others, make sure you do a self-introspection, and clear your path before you blame others. For years, I was constantly feeling sorry for myself and was stuck in a valley of darkness with no hope in sight. It was not until I took responsibility for my life that my circumstances changed.

We may have all the potential to share with the world, but without focus, your abilities are useless. Setting goals is like a measuring stick that we can use to track our progress; it also creates accountability for one's self. We are bombarded with many distractions, year in and year out, but if we implement goal setting, it keeps us locked in and not distracted by every wind that passes. Setting goals also helps in putting procrastination on the right track. Many bad habits can join forces to leave us stagnant and mentally bankrupt, and we must overcome these forces by feeding the things that aid in improving our lives. The things we dismissed as simply small defects, can add up over time and be to our own detriment.

Trauma can leave us with a lack of motivation, but goal setting helps to inspire us and brings meaning to our lives. Focus is the driving force behind motivation. The greatest tragedy of life doesn't lie in not reaching your goals, but rather having no goals to reach. The biggest lie we tell ourselves is that goals are meaningless. I recall the year 2004, when I embarked on setting goals because I was tired of my life. I felt that my life was going around in circles, with no real purpose. This was my first real attempt at setting long and short-term goals. I was specific about what I wanted to accomplish. The most successful year of my life was 2004, and it started a method that is contagious to this day. There is a proven method that should be implemented in goal setting, and that is the SMART goal template: Smart, Manageable, Attainable, Realistic, and Time specific. Follow this method and pave the way to a successful future. We were not created just to occupy space, but rather to be productive individuals. Never allow these unseemly little glitches to take over your life and slowly eat away at your ability to be aware of the hindrances to your progress.

Notes

Chapter 6

Own Your Box

Many people are not comfortable with the body they were born in, so they spend thousands of dollars trying to be someone they are not. We disguise ourselves to fit into different clichés, and try to live it up like the "Joneses." Hidden not far from view is emptiness and vanity, but we put up this façade to blind others from our empty existence. We are afraid of silence because we do not want to face the truth about ourselves. We are owners of our destiny. Working in partnership with God's supernatural power and our abilities, we can be a force to be reckoned with. Our focus should be on chartering the course of molding our character and working every day to improve ourselves.

We are as strong as our inner ability to decipher the things that are necessary to build our future. When we take ownership of our "BOX," we are building our inner strength. A certain degree of inner strength will give you the confidence and the assertiveness to deal with the difficulties of life, as well as the way to interact with others. It can also help with one's concentration level. Our minds can act like the wind, tossing to and fro; but instead of drifting whenever it wants, we can choose to redirect our focus on what is important in life. We can also do this by practicing concentration exercises, and this would strengthen the attention and power of our minds, and therefore give us control of our thoughts, actions, and our lives.

It is important for us to accept our flaws; we are wasting years trying to be what we are not. Accept yourself and your past, and this will aid you in accepting your destiny. We need to unconditionally embrace every part of ourselves—the good, the bad, and the ugly. Everyone loves to know that they are valued and appreciated; however, acceptance begins with one's ability to first accept oneself. We can accept ourselves by accepting our present realities, and bearing in mind that struggles and disappointments are all part of our reality. It is easy for us to look in the mirror and point out all our insecurities, but we need to start counting all the positives in our lives. Sometimes we tend to forget due to the pressures of life or the many things that distract our minds. Make a list of your strengths, the things you are good at, the values that you hold, and your accomplishments. By doing these things, you can realize your strengths, which in turn will help you improve your attitude toward yourself.

Our souls live in our bodies, and whatever we feed our bodies, we also feed our souls. Our souls not only evolve in the natural realm but, most importantly, in the spiritual realm as well. Many of us are disconnected from our souls, and so we walk around less aware of what is happening around us. COVID-19 has already taken many things from us, especially our freedom, and has created chaos, grief, etc. in our world. What our current situation can teach us is to build our inner immunity against the interference of outside forces. We have the power to create our own paradise, even in the midst of the pandemic. Aligning with your soul can help you live a more conscious and mindful life, since it is the most powerful force that we have as individuals. Find ways to connect with your soul, especially during this pandemic. This will bring things into the right perspective and quiet your troubled mind.

> *"There is definitely more left in you than what those negative thoughts are forcing you to believe. Quitting on yourself should never be an option in your life. Success is your true destiny; keep pushing until something very rewarding happens."*
> – Edmond Mbiaka

Appreciate the Power of Slow

When trying to heal from trauma, it is imperative to not be hard on yourself if the road to healing is slow. We are living in a fast-paced world, where people believe in getting things done at a fast pace. The healing process should be a slow and reflective experience; we should never rush the process. There are many phases in the recovery process from trauma, and "slow" does not symbolize ineffectiveness. At different stages, you may observe the changes in your body and mind as they adjust to the different changes that are occurring. Your body is undergoing major reconstruction, and it is at this stage that one should exercise patience and understanding with oneself. Remember, you are picking up the broken pieces of your life and rebuilding a stronger you.

"Rome was not built in a day." Every good thing takes time and much effort. The recovery process should always aim to focus on the moment, working with what you have and trying to improve the quality of your life daily. We may think that we have control over many things, but one thing we do not have control over is "TIME." Time flies faster than we imagine, but we are in charge of the time allotted to us and, with God as our pilot, all things are possible. A whole deal of motivation, concentration, self-control, and many other things form the foundation with which we can all prevent roadblocks and self-sabotage. We must not fear the enemy or outside forces we think are working against us, but rather fear our inner inability to deal with ourselves.

Practice becomes routine, and helps to form new habits. As you progress, never become complacent; this can slow the growth process and can hinder the path to achieve true success. Remember that habits form character, and if we are trying to recover from past hurts, we must avoid bad habits at all cost. Avoiding them will eliminate all forms of self-inflicted wounds. Much time should be spent on establishing a new foundation, one that is molded from the experiences of your past, to build a brighter future.

Escaping Ugly

> *"Everyone has a right to have a present and future that are not completely dominated and dictated by the past."*
> – Karen Saakvitne

As a child, I was always fascinated by the story about the race between the rabbit and the turtle. By nature, turtles are slow, and it would serve as a laughable and almost impossible challenge for a turtle to find something that is slower than him. In the end, however, the turtle won the race. Being slow is not necessarily a bad thing, once you are aware of all the odds that are stacked against you. The rabbit had more to lose than the turtle, but he was being overconfident in his abilities and underestimated his opponent. The healing process is not a race. It is only through endurance that we can overcome the good and bad days to see the rainbow ahead. We are never alone on our journeys. God is always with us; he is the one propelling us forward to discover our true selves.

Say "NO" to Internalizing Oppression

Internalized oppression (also known as self-directed oppression) happens when a marginalized or oppressed population begins to accept and act on stereotypes and other inaccurate beliefs related to it. On a personal level, internalized oppression happens when we impose limits on ourselves in pursuit of safety. For example, a woman feels that she is a loser and is incapable of achieving her goals, due to negative remarks that others said to her. Oppression can come in many forms, and we can be oppressed for various reasons, due to race, culture, sexual orientation, gender, etc. Sometimes we unconsciously buy into the negative messages that are propagated about who we are, and then we begin to internalize the oppression that we experienced. Many of us are not aware of the many powers working against us that are due mostly to our social class.

We learn that having certain traits, being a member of a particular group, and being who we are, is not good enough or is not desirable. The sad reality is that we can even learn to hate our traits and ourselves. This can further lead to us hurting other members in our communities, who share many similarities with us. Internalized oppression not only affects us, but it can be filter into our relationships and, if not handled properly, can destroy families, cultures, and communities. Many of us are not aware of how internalized oppression may exist within us, so we may not even grasp the concept of how to control its effects on our lives. It is vital for us to understand that we were not born hating ourselves; we learned it based on our experiences. Therefore, we can also unlearn it.

We gravitate to everything around us and measure ourselves against a certain standard where we think we are coming up short. Society puts us into different roles, and dictates rules and certain norms to which we are expected to adhere. Although there are many forms of oppression around us, the one that is the most detrimental is the one where we inflict scars on ourselves, due to the lies we tell ourselves. Social media can tell us one thing, and society can tell us another, but what we choose to believe is the most vital.

As a child growing up, I was in an environment where the cultivation of bananas was a huge part of my early upbringing. I hated everything about bananas: the smell, the taste, and most importantly, the impact it had on the younger generation. Many children never aspired for higher education because they were brainwashed into believing that "farming doesn't require a high level of education." Most children only attained a primary education because banana production was more important than an education. I have seen many promising futures destroyed due to this concept. I made a promise not to fall into that trap. I recall sitting in my father's banana field, dreaming of a life outside of that narrow existence. I made a promise to myself that this would never be my position, and even if I was forced to, my outer existence would never take away my inner reality. We need to dream again and create something better than what we are experiencing right now. Be hopeful about the future, and even if the odds are stacked against us, we should always persevere.

"Reactive people are driven by feelings, by circumstances, by conditions, by their environment. Proactive people are driven by values—carefully thought about, selected, and internalized values."
– Stephen Covey

Feed Your Soul Too

Our souls will never go away; they are a huge part of who we are; however, if we fail to nurture them, we are doing ourselves a huge injustice. Life happens, and there are many things that are beyond our control, but notwithstanding what is happening in our world, we need to find things to feed our souls. We invest so much in things that are temporal, yet we fail to use the same energy to invest in ourselves. Homes have now been transformed into havens for work, school, and recreational activities. Many individuals are now getting used to the "new normal." We have been given a second chance to undo our wrongs, spend time with the people that matter most to us, and replenish our spiritual lives. The soul has a blueprint that we need to follow and adhere to, but we cannot adhere to it if we are unaware of the power that lies in accessing the forces within.

The soul's journey to wholeness must start with an understanding and implementation of the principles that govern the soul. Many of us do not understand who we are, because we allow the world to tell us who we should be. We allow circumstances and past experiences to dictate who we should be, and so we go along, like sheep to the slaughterhouse. The saddest state we can find ourselves in is to be living in the past while we are in the present. We are known by the names given to us and are associated with the families we were born into, but we are far from understanding who we are as individuals. We need to raise our level of awareness by learning how to navigate the forces in our lives that are working against us, such as fear. It is something that is constructed and forces us to remain in our comfort zones.

When we fail to recognize that things are crippling our progress, we are feeding negative behaviors and allowing the circle to repeat itself. You may realize that your life is stagnant, and you are upset at the world for no reason known to you; that is the time when practiced behavior has taken over your mind. The process of becoming whole is often likened to the evolution of a butterfly: from a cocoon (which to the naked eye appears less pleasant and more unknown) to a beautiful butterfly. We are nothing without our past, and so it is necessary to go through unpleasant circumstances in order to be transformed into beautiful human beings. Tapping into the forces of the soul will unveil the many talents that we are sometimes not aware of. The most awkward moment for many is when they are asked to introduce themselves and describe things that make them unique. Most people are not aware of their strengths and talents. If we are not in tune with our souls, we become strangers in our own bodies.

> *"When someone dies, their body lies lifeless,*
> *and they are not aware of what is happening around them.*
> *But I believe the worst death is one where an individual is alive*
> *but fails to live up to their true potential."*
> *– Deloris Gardner*

We are not truly living if we have not discovered our purpose on earth. We are robbing ourselves and humanity if we fail to know the reason for our existence and willingly share our talents for the better good of others. The universe works in accordance with our souls, to give signs and interpretations to let us know if we are on the right path.

> *"When she transformed into a butterfly,*
> *the caterpillars spoke not of her beauty but of her weirdness.*
> *They wanted her to change back to what she had always been.*
> *But she had wings."*
> *– Dean Jackson*

The butterfly didn't form overnight; she was once a vulnerable caterpillar, then in a cocoon, and finally a beautiful butterfly. She could now enjoy the freedom of flying and living up to her true potential, but she wouldn't have had the opportunity to enjoy such freedom if she hadn't endured hardship.

Resensitization – Bouncing Back after Trauma

The longer we live, the more inevitable it is for us to experience trauma. In fact, many people are experiencing trauma because of this pandemic. Trauma is a feeling of distress or a disturbing event that overwhelms an individual's ability to cope, causes feelings of helplessness, and diminishes their sense of self. Usually, trauma occurs suddenly, which can create shock in the initial stage for many trauma survivors. This pandemic is traumatic for all of us, since we were not prepared for the impact it is having on our mental, social, psychological, and emotional well-being. For many who have lost loved ones because of this pandemic, the damage is even more severe, especially because of lack of closure. We need to develop the ability to not only cope but thrive. We can make the most of our present situation and look on the brighter side of this pandemic.

We have the potential to bounce back from this pandemic—we are blessed to be alive, and this is the first step of hope. The very air that we breathe, we took for granted; but now it is the air that can be detrimental to our health and others. Many people are feeling overwhelmed and confused right now, and they may not be able to describe how they are feeling. When people are traumatized, they usually feel unsafe in their own bodies, and they may feel that their interior is slowly falling apart. What is happening to us is a natural reaction to trauma, and these are warning signs for us to take action to avoid potentially more severe mishaps. We have the power to train our brains to refocus on something positive whenever negative thoughts flood our minds. Let us not wait until this pandemic is over, to work on regulating our emotions—by then, it may be too late. We must seize every moment for healing and reviving our souls.

The art of resensitizing our brains after trauma is a process that should be ongoing. Don't ignore the signs you are experiencing in your body/mind; these are warning signs that we should take action quickly. When our bodies are disconnected from us, we are in turn disconnected from the world. We are facing a worldwide global crisis, which for many could well be their first experience of something of this magnitude. Many who were once optimistic are now pessimistic about facing the future—their rubber has hit the road, and it is a painful sight. How can one be hopeful in these troubling times, you may ask? It is all about choices. Yes, we have a huge role to play in the affairs that govern our lives. What we say and think, matters hugely in the outcome after this pandemic. Since we are not in control of the affairs of the universe, the best we can do for ourselves is to accept our fate and make the best of it.

Many are looking at this as their biggest nightmare, and they wish to awake from their sleep, while others are using it as an opportunity to grow. YES!! We can grow through this pandemic. Many are playing the blaming game: World leaders are pinning the blame on China. Instead of this current crisis uniting the world, some countries have become selfish by withholding or refusing to share much needed medical supplies. President Trump was not even sure what to say during an interview. He made this useless statement: "People are dying that have never died before." We need not to wait until this is finished to bounce back; we should implement this in our regular exercise routine. On the road to resensitization, we must be willing to work daily on keeping track of our feelings and how it affects our emotions. Furthermore, let us emerge on the other side of pain as people who are more creative in availing themselves and finding new connections and different ways of interacting, whether on Zoom or other outlets.

Don't Be Afraid of Pushing the Limit

There is a limit to everything in life; however, sometimes we must be willing to push past the limit to become overcomers. I am not asking anyone to do something illegal, but what I am saying is to move past the barriers we have set for ourselves. Sometimes, unconsciously, we may not be aware of these barriers, because we have become so familiar with these things that they can become a normal way of functioning. We have become "little," like a child afraid of their own shadow. We are comfortable rolling with the punches life throws at us, without questioning the reasons, and we never fight back. We are meant to push the limits. Early this year, I wanted to get back into shape, so I started going to the gym; but to get to my end goal, I must be willing to push the limit of my comfort zone. We may never know our limits unless we can push them ourselves, and only through this can we discover our full potential.

We are somewhat limited because of COVID-19, because there are many restrictions that are placed on us. When you test your limits, you discover different paths that can lead to a variety of avenues that you can explore. To thrive in these uncertain times, you need to find a way to press through the setbacks and create your own paradise. Refrain from allowing your mind to become lazy. Many individuals are now at home with nothing much to do, and they are repeating the same routine every day. This can become quite boring. Life is an end product of problems, big and small. It is continuous, and we are never truly free from problems. It is even more difficult now because what we are facing is not what we created, but rather it is something that we had absolutely no clue about.

The good thing about human nature is our ability to make quick adjustments during times of turmoil. This pandemic is not going anywhere anytime soon, so we need to respond quickly and positively to overcome. At this very moment, we are not sure when this pandemic is going to be over, and we are constantly living a life of uncertainty. We need to practice not thinking that far ahead, and learn to live in the moment and appreciate what we have now. Making quick adjustments in order to accommodate a present setback is going to be a major factor in how we overcome this ordeal. We can use this experience as an opportunity for positive personal growth. The moment is extremely difficult for all of us because we are without emotional support; and in addition, all community services are currently closed.

Finding creative ways of accessing vital mental health resources is necessary. Researchers studying people exposed to events such as accidents, war zone deployment, serious illness, or bereavement, have found that social support and relationships with others, in the time period following the event, are key predictors of psychological recovery. Having social support and relationships with others is an integral part in bouncing back better and stronger after trauma; however, we are without the much needed help that we seek, due to restrictions. With this in mind, finding creative ways of accessing vital mental health resources is necessary. During this stressful time, we can find time to enjoy the simple pleasures of life, such as taking nature walks when the weather is good, and investing in our spiritual lives. Let us exercise gratitude when realizing how close we have come to dying, and be grateful that God has given us another chance to live. Surviving this traumatic experience may represent to us a second chance to rebuild our lives and implement the lessons we need to learn.

Notes

Chapter 7

What We Can Learn from COVID-19

During the writing of this book, COVID-19 came along and completely changed the normalcy we took for granted and didn't take the time to truly appreciate. I was totally thrown off guard, as many of us were, and did not know how to make the necessary adjustments to life. There were days, even weeks, when I thought it was a dream and that I would eventually wake up and breathe a sigh of relief. To make matters worse, I wanted to give up my dream of being a published author. My dream was stronger than my present reality, so I pressed on every day notwithstanding my feelings and what was happening around the world. Our brains are not programmed or have a set method of how to react to shock, and many people are still trying to process what the new normal looks like. In fact, many individuals who have underlying health issues, are the most vulnerable.

Many individuals have taken up the mantle of being their brother's keeper, while others have become more selfish by not thinking about the needs of others. When the brain is trying to make sense of shock, one may experience a series of mixed emotions. One moment, you are happy, sad, angry, confused, etc., and you cannot express your true feelings. Many people are asking the question: "What will life be like after COVID? We have seen, around the world, where many individuals have even resorted to suicide. The mental health of many should be maintained daily, and one should find someone to talk to about their true feelings. For many, the restrictions make it almost impossible to find that one-on-one social support to ease the hurt.

All is not lost!! There is still HOPE. This pandemic has unraveled the puzzle of the true meaning of life. I recently read about the life of a famous Nollywood actor who, for 10 years, wanted to spend his birthday with his family. His many gigs abroad never allowed him time at home with his family. However, it was during this period that he was able to fly home and spend his birthday at home with his family. In a conversation with a gentleman, he mentioned that it was the first time he had taken a vacation in 10 years. His life, which once consisted of busy commutes, long hours at work, and even working two jobs, was now a life of leisure.

The earth is singing praises: There is clear water in the canals in Venice; there are blue skies over Delhi; and wild animals are roaming boldly in locked-down cities. The irony is that we are locked inside while the animals are free to roam. COVID-19 is teaching us the importance of family time; we are learning the true meaning of life. God is giving us all another opportunity to spend time in his word, to make a final decision to follow him with all our hearts, minds, and souls. "For we should not fear what can destroy the body, but we should be more concerned about what destroys both body and soul." Let us focus more on securing our souls, and be counted in the numbers spending eternity with our Creator.

Let us make full use of the time we have at home with our families, make amends for past wrongs, and totally work on eliminating bad habits. Use this time for true reflection, self-care, and self-improvement. We may NEVER get this opportunity again to do the things that are important. We have a chance to do something extraordinary. As we head out of this pandemic, we can change the world. Create a world of love: a world where we are kinder to each other; a world where we are kind, no matter our class, race, sexual orientation, religion, or job. COVID-19 is breaking down the barriers of class, race, etc. We are learning new ways of surviving every day, and we are also learning more about our families, communities, and the world. Let us all strive to be kind and to learn ways of spreading love and kindness.

What We Can Learn from COVID-19

Stand in the Storm

The outbreak of COVID-19 has touched all parts of the world's population. For most of us, all of life as we know it has changed significantly, and to add insult to injury, many are facing joblessness due to the downturn in the economy. Many people are living in fear of the unknown every day; they are living every moment hoping that things will get better and not worse. For many, it is an extended vacation; others are concerned about their finances and daily well-being. Storms normally come without warning, so it is impossible to prepare for tragedies. We are forced to adopt to a new reality, with an empty toolkit, and we are learning as we proceed through our daily lives. I have never seen anyone putting the welcome mat out to welcome a storm; we instead look at it as a disturbance in our lives.

Storms are designed to do many important things in our lives. Like COVID-19, storms teach us valuable lessons about ourselves, others, and the lives we have created. Storms bring people and communities closer together. Storms bring out the heroic qualities in many of us. In 1995, when I was a teenager, there was a major hurricane that totally devastated the Caribbean islands of Antigua and Barbuda. We had to seek shelter in a school close to our home, and it was during this time, while interacting with various individuals in the shelter, that we developed a spirit of comradeship that bound us together as fellow human beings. This spirit of comradeship played a pivotal role in helping to ease the pain as well as unite strangers together. There are so many things that separate us, but when we are faced with a tragedy, we learn to put aside prejudices and work together for a common good.

Not all storms come to break us; some come to mold us into better human beings. Many of us are afraid of change—even in our lives, we would choose to stay stagnant, because that is our safe place. Our comfort zone will never propel us to grow, so this season of change has taken its toll on our mental, social, and emotional well-being. We need to become more adaptable to change in order to survive this period of our lives. Storms are going to occur more frequently, since it has been determined that the world economy is not going to get better anytime soon. Maybe we are heading into a recession, and if this is the case, how prepared are we? Let us be mindful not to take nothing for granted.

Our wardrobes and expensive cars are being wasted, with nowhere to go. We have invested so much into our outer existence, and we neglect things that help to improve our inner being. Many people work to make a living but have not learned how to make a life. They work to acquire riches to impress others, but they are shallow inside. Many are hurting in different ways due to COVID-19, but the greatest hurt that many are experiencing is loneliness. They have invested more time in proving to others that they are enough, but now there are no outlets for which to show off or dress up. All that they ever possessed was vanity. What is most important is that every person works out their soul's salvation between themselves and God. The most precious, most valuable pieces of jewelry were formed through the most difficult conditions. Likewise, some of the strongest people that I have ever met are those who have constantly been exposed to the storms of life. In my own experience, it was my darkest moments that helped to build my character. We need to totally eradicate the microwave mindset, because when something comes easy without much effort, it does not build our immunity. We are not supposed to walk out of a storm the way we came in; storms are meant to make us better individuals, and humbled by a higher power that controls the universe.

> *"And when the storm is over, you won't remember how you made it through, how you managed to survive. You won't even be sure whether the storm is really over. But one thing is certain, when you come out of the storm, you won't be the same person who walked in. That's what this storm's all about."*
> – Haruki Murakami

Adjust to Your New Reality

Many people are living in the past, wishing and hoping on a star that has already changed location. We went to bed one night and woke up in the morning to a different world, a new state of existence. Some of us are yet to accept what is happening in the world as it is now. The faster we can accept this new way of life, the faster we can learn ways of not only coping but thriving. Yes, we can still strive amid this pandemic. After trauma, I was stuck in the self-denial stage for a long time, so it played a huge role in prolonging my progress. Once we are willing to accept our present reality, it is the first step to self-improvement and success.

The entire world is experiencing a collaborative trauma—for many, the death of loves ones—and the many restrictions that are in place are making it impossible for us to reach out to others. We are created to be social beings, and this time away from many social settings is taking its toll on our mental and spiritual lives. To accept your new reality, it is necessary to embark on the path of desensitization, which is the process of coming back after trauma. Many may be experiencing emotions right now that are unexplainable. We are still in the early stages of this pandemic, so it is difficult to fathom what the latter part will look like, or the devastation it is going to have on the entire human race. One thing is certain: The world will never be the same again!! It will take years for normalcy to return. Everywhere, anxiety is running high. Community centers that once provided a safe haven for many, are now closed, with no opening dates in sight.

Many people are wondering what can emerge after COVID-19. Many may have started this year with many plans they wanted to accomplish for 2020. Now life appears to be meaningless, without direction, and day-to-day living can seem like torture. We need not look on the negative side of COVID-19, but focus on the fact that we are alive, and God is still supplying our daily needs. God has spared our lives, but many are not as fortunate as we are, to be alive. Find things to focus your energy on: "What is the reason God is keeping me alive, and for what purpose am I here?" We have been given another chance to live every day; why not make it count?

In the midst of adversity, we can choose to be of help to humanity, or become a liability. During the early part of this pandemic, we have seen the worse side of humanity, such as the apocalypse-like behavior of purchasing everything in the grocery stores, with no regard for others, which was a huge shock. This is a time when we should show more empathy toward each other, because all of us are sharing the same trauma. This is an opportunity for the human species to be supportive of one another and grow, or to become fearful and become further disassociated from each other. We need to get back to being our brother's keeper. We may not have the opportunity to socialize right now, due to the social distancing restrictions, but we can find ways of connecting. The growing numbers are telling us that people are still not willing to trade a moment of freedom for the greater good of others. Many are going out unnecessarily and thus putting themselves and others at risk. Since we were not created to live on this earth forever, let us do our best to play an integral role for those we come in contact with. We are all hurting, and we are all sharing the same pain—some worse than others—and the time has come to be the change we want to see in the world. Let us not use COVID-19 as an excuse to be rude and inconsiderate.

"Life is a series of natural and spontaneous changes.
Don't resist them; that only creates sorrow. Let reality be reality.
Let things flow naturally forward in whatever way they like."
– Lao Tzu

This Too Shall Pass

My favorite song, especially after my traumatic experience, was "This Too Shall Pass," by Yolanda Adams. In my darkest moments, I found peace and strength in the words of this song. I am reminding my readers once again that whatever is happening in your life right now, remember: "This too shall pass." We are not meant to go through pain forever; everything is for a time and a season. In the modern sense, it means that everything that happens in our lives that would tend to throw us off course is transient, since nothing lasts forever. In life, change is inevitable. We readily accept the good as we do the bad, because not every storm is meant to break us; some are sent to mold us into better human beings. The faster we can embrace life's setbacks, the sooner we can recover and become better.

Abraham Lincoln, in an address to the Wisconsin State Agricultural Society, in 1859, said: *"It is said an Eastern monarch once charged his wise men to invent him a sentence to be ever in view, and which should be true and appropriate in all times and situations. They presented him the words, 'And this too, shall pass away.'"* In the harshest of times, we can bear in mind that once we are living, we must pass through difficulties. The world is now facing the biggest crisis of the 21st century, and many people are searching for answers. The world's leaders are just as puzzled as the man on the street. The big and powerful superpower, the United States of America, who once supplied aid to the world, is now falling short of medical supplies. We have entered a phase where anxiety is running high, and death tolls are rising every second of the day. We have seen, around the world, where many are surrendering their lives to God. They have come to realize that God is their creator, and only in him can they find peace and security amidst this "killer monster."

There is another monster lurking in the silent darkness, ready to unleash something more devastating than COVID-19: the monster of mental illnesses, due to lack of social support, and lack of an outlet for grieving families to see their loved ones before and after the cold hand of death takes them away. In Canada, during this period of social isolation, many women have lost their lives through partner violence. Many are forced to coexist in unhealthy relationships without an outlet to vent their frustration or, most importantly, to get the help that they need. The impact from this pandemic has forced parents to enter into uncharted territory, having to decipher the best course of action for themselves and their families. Children are frustrated and need answers as to why everything is closed, and why they must stay indoors every day. Additionally, we must get used to long lines and empty shelves at every essential store, and wearing masks and gloves. This has become the new normal.

How we overcome this new way of existing is hugely based on our ability to make quick adjustments and implement positive coping mechanisms. We are not alone!! There is still hope. We just need to become more creative. With the vast improvement in social media, we can find useful resources. Furthermore, we need to retain our spiritual lives. Let us not only remember God in times of trouble, but recommit our lives to serving him wholeheartedly for the rest of our lives. If you are reading this, you have survived some of your worst days; be encouraged and hold firm. *"Your best stories will come from your struggles. The seed of your successes is in your failures. The praises will be birthed through your pains. Keep standing; I have never seen a storm last forever."* Worry is a waste of energy and a stealer of time. Live in the present with gratitude for what you have now, with anticipation of what is to come.

Rebuild a Solid Foundation

We can only fix something that is broken, and rebuilding always comes after great devastation. After a storm, one must embark on the process of rebuilding, because your foundation, or even the entire structure, may have crumbled or been shaken. Rebuilding is not the easiest thing to venture into; it requires time and patience, and we can also grow in the process. The focus, during and after trauma, should be on rebuilding our emotional, psychological, and spiritual foundation. We have spent a large part of our lives investing in things that are temporary, things that would eventually rot, but now is the time to invest in our eternal foundation, which cannot gather mold, and will never fade away.

Rebuilding a solid foundation that will not crumble from life's many storms, should be anchored on the rock of "Jesus." He is the only one that can keep us safe and secure through the many disasters that we endure. When one embarks on building a foundation, it is not easy at first; but nothing worth having is ever easy. However, if you stick with it, with daily steps and a belief in yourself, you will build a rock-solid foundation. Over time, it will get easier, because you will have built up your foundation blocks one by one, with care. Then when the storms of life come along, you may be shaken but not blown over. You will have developed the tenacity to keep moving ahead, swimming through the high waves, with slow, steady movement until you can find some stability to keep you grounded.

You have fought through the worst of days, so give yourself permission to embark on a journey of enjoying the best days of your life. Rebuilding comes with more low days than good days, but when you look at the promise of something better than what you had before, that is the motivation that dispels your inner critic. When we reach a place of acceptance of personal loss or tragedy, it is then that we experience true liberation. In addition, when we embrace suffering as part of life's experience that we cannot control, then we are opening ourselves to learn some of life's greatest lessons. Many relish in the idea of newness, but they are not willing to endure the devastation that comes with the storm, in order to get to the calm. As with most experiences, you can learn and grow from what has happened during your storms. Even though it may not resonate now, what you have gone through has made you stronger, not weaker. Sure, you may feel weak, and even hopeless at times, but there is an inner strength and courage far beyond what you can imagine.

Trauma is a life-changing event that knocks you off balance and makes you question everything that was once an asset to your development. Everything you have ever known about yourself is tossed out the window, and you are left looking at the stranger staring at you in the mirror. Suddenly, you question who you are—your goals and dreams—and your dreams seem like a fleeting image that once had meaning. Trauma disrupts your path and leaves in its wake a high heap of debris of mass proportion. Hitting rock bottom is not the end; in fact, it is the best position in which to start. Everything that is meant to last should be built from the bottom up. Again, when rebuilding and dealing with trauma, healing will not happen quickly. Remember to be patient and gentle with yourself while allowing the process to unfold. Do not be harsh with yourself; you have already experienced enough. Use the opportunity, when you are in the process of rebuilding, to become the chief architect of your life's plan. Incorporate some of the attributes you were lacking, and build a foundation that you will be proud of. Make it grand, make it great, and live out your deepest heart's desires.

Mind Over Matter

Mind over matter is a phrase that is familiar to many of us, but what does it really mean? It is a situation in which an individual can control a physical condition or problem by using the mind. If one is able to develop the ability to control their mind through the many scenes of life, then they will have mastered the power to live a peaceful life, regardless of what is happening in the world. We should all strive to look at the good in every situation. We can triumph over physical hindrances, through the power of the mind. The thoughts we allow in our minds can either be our weapons *for* or *against* the world, and they can also be weapons against ourselves. We are confined to the walls that we build for ourselves. If you are reading this, it is because you are alive. Break down the walls you have built in your mind, and watch your circumstances change for the better.

We sometimes throw this phrase around with absolutely no regard to what it means, or knowing that it can change our mindset in life. I can recall reading a book by Napoleon Hill, which completely elevated my life and, even today, is the reason behind my determination to conquer my inner space. This beautiful book, *Think and Grow Rich*, rewired my brain for success in every aspect of my life. The mind is the most powerful weapon that we possess as human beings. Our ability to capitalize on every opportunity to be the stewards of it, while closing the lid, with no avenue for accountability for oneself, can be classified as a self-induced coma while being alive in the body. According to various studies, people only use 10% of their brain power. This simply means that if we are willing to unlock the remaining 90%, we can move from the valley of sameness, to unprecedented success. We tend to think that we are okay because those around us are in the same bracket as we are, but unless we are willing to enlarge our territories, then it would be impossible to think differently.

"Mind over matter" teaches us how mind patterns can influence our physical reality. Everything, good or bad, starts in the mind and becomes practice, which would eventually lead to habits. We have the power to choose the thoughts and feelings that create our physical life experiences. All that matters is contained within the mind, and when we can use the mind to decipher the vital issues of our existence, we are enculturating a precedent that would be the blueprint for future successes. Despite the matters that surround us every day, we can choose the thoughts and feelings that give substance to what we perceive. Thoughts are the DNA of the universe. What we send out in the universe speaks volumes of who we are and how we think. Over time, our thoughts can either make or break us.

With so many things happening in our world, cultivating positive thoughts has become even more difficult. The devastating effect of COVID-19, on our mental health, is becoming more difficult by the second; and in addition, we are facing yet another problem. Racism has claimed the lives of many young black men. The recent death of George Floyd started many protests around the globe. Pain is temporary; it may last a day, weeks, or years, but it will eventually subside, and something else will take its place. If I quit, however, it lasts forever. That surrender, even the smallest act of giving up, stays with us. So, when you feel like quitting, ask yourself what you would rather live with. Pain and turmoil seem to be a common phenomenon in 2020. We are not sure what is coming next, but what I do know is that we still have the power within us to control our utter existence. My grandmother always says that she can live with the devil in hell. You have to make the relevant adjustment to life as you know it NOW, and use your mind in a positive way and for the betterment of others.

Notes

Chapter 8

Acceptance – The First Stage of Healing

Many individuals are searching for healing from past hurts, yet they are not willing to embark on the first stage, which is acceptance. Acceptance sets the stage for the healing process to take place. When we experience devastating loss, such as the death of a loved one, we experience grief. The stages that are associated with grief usually follow a certain pattern: denial, anger, depression, and acceptance. Based on one's level of grief, the pattern may differ. We sometimes have the wrong notion of acceptance. It is not the dismissing of what happened; it is learning to be okay with the way things are. As difficult as things may be, being able to adapt and accept whatever life throws at us is key to finding happiness. We cannot control the affairs of the world, and we certainly cannot control how things will work out for us, no matter how good a person we are. What we can control is how we can choose to make lemonade from the lemons that life throws at us. If you are constantly dwelling on the past, and wishing and hoping for what was, then you are depriving yourself of the right to move forward.

Acceptance was one of the hardest pills for me to swallow. I had the notion that if I accepted something, then I was saying in a sense that it was okay for the abuse to happen. Furthermore, I was of the belief that I was letting the perpetrator off the hook. So, for years, I was wallowing in self-pity and would replay, like a broken record, something that happened years before. When I finally snapped out of it, the damage was already done: My physical, mental, psychological, and emotional state took a severe beating, which took me a longer time to get back on track. My anxiety level was so high that I was afraid of leaving my apartment. The ambulance and medical personnel were frequent visitors at my home. I developed an irregular heartbeat, and I lost so much weight that my clothes could have fit around me twice. In my opinion, I subconsciously refused to accept my situation, because that was my safe place—a place where I could hide out so I would not be accountable to anyone, even to myself. It was a place that I was familiar with, even if it was unhealthy and a bad recipe for my mental health. This was my excuse to remain unproductive and stagnant.

Acceptance is the greatest therapeutic tool we can give to ourselves on the road to a full recovery. It is not going to be perfect, and we may fall along the way, or wander over into the path of hurt. However, if you are willing to embrace it with an open mind, it would serve you well. Sometimes we can become so consumed with an image we have in our minds of how we want the outcome to be, that we miss the incredible journey of seeing the scars being healed, and really seeing our lives transforming around us. Acceptance helps you to be intentional and totally present mentally to experience all the amazing things happening in your life in the moment, instead of fixating on the things you don't have or the life you once had. Pain can become a place that you are comfortable with, since it was once a reminder of normalcy or things that are familiar.

Acceptance not only helps you feel happy, but it can also help heal you in certain circumstances. When we accept, we are releasing the tensions of hurt and pain, and giving our bodies the opportunity to heal and replenish themselves. Furthermore, we are giving ourselves the freedom to heal.

> *"Acceptance looks like a passive state, but in reality,*
> *it brings something entirely new into this world.*
> *That peace, a subtle energy vibration, is consciousness."*
> *– Eckhart Tolle*

Enduring Your Night

In the early stages after my trauma, I could compare night to a hot meal that was often served cold. It was one of the most difficult periods for me: I had many sleepless nights and would have regular occurrences of nightmares, and even some "daymares" as well. Since night can be symbolic of darkness and silence, it can become unbearable when left alone with your thoughts or being reminded of that bleak time in your experience. Thank God, I didn't resort to taking sleeping pills or any form of medication. Night can pose as a reminder of that dark period in your life; in addition, the silence can also remind you of the helpless attacks from the perpetrator. Sometimes many people may try to force us to heal, with the belief that we should just "get over it already," or "let it go." There is no magic wand that can be waved to make everything disappear like it never happened. Many people have not yet fully grasped their individual trauma, yet they are pressured to heal prematurely. You are entitled to your time of healing, whatever that may look like for you. I know, for me, it gets easier with time, but it is something that is forever a huge part of my unique experience.

Because you are having difficulties surviving your night, does not mean that you are weak or incapable of healing. This is all part of the "surviving trauma" experience. However, once we accept our situation, we become more accountable to ourselves, which in turn creates a positive outlook. Trauma survivors are often highly motivated people. Many of the strong attributes we cultivated are due hugely to our experience. Many are conditioned to be hyperaware, resilient, strong, and hypervigilant, out of survival. We subconsciously developed and mastered the art of hiding and storing pain in the darkest part of the mind, and are afraid of bringing it to light because of not wanting to deal with it. For me, one of my biggest coping mechanisms was to disassociate myself from the pain, with the notion that, mentally, it would go away or ease the pain in the moment. Trauma survivors are often overworked because the brain is working overtime to deal with flashbacks, which increases anxiety levels, and which makes it harder for survivors as compared to someone without trauma. That is why many survivors often feel lazy and unproductive, and can even believe that they are stuck in a rut that they cannot get out of.

Night doesn't have to be a scary place. Once we condition our minds to embark on the healing process, and put acceptance on the top of the list, we are laying the groundwork for miracles to happen. In Elie Wiesel's recollection of his experience in a Nazi death camp, in his book, *Night*, it was symbolic to him, of the darkest period of his existence. He was brainwashed into targeting his anger on his father instead of the SS officers. This can also be the way we have been programmed to lash out at ourselves instead of channeling the anger to the perpetrator. We have thought, over time, that we deserved what happened to us, and that we are useless. Over a period of time, we believed it, and so it dominated everything that we did. When the body is overstimulated, the brain is flooded with neurochemicals that keep us awake, such as epinephrine and adrenaline, making it difficult to wind down at the end of the day. We can endure our night by confronting our fears. Things will become easier with time, and when you are healing, be forgiving of yourself, and remind yourself that it is okay to not be okay. Every day is not the same, and over time you will rejoice in every small victory, and climax it into great miracles.

"Even a happy life cannot be without a measure of darkness, and the word happy would lose its meaning if it were not balanced with sadness. It is far better to take things as they come along, with patience and equanimity."
– Carl Jung

When the Rainbow Does Not Have a Silver Lining

We sometimes use the idiomatic expression, "every cloud has a silver lining," to bring hope and comfort in the midst of difficulty. It helps in soothing an otherwise desperate or gloomy situation.

Whether we refer to it as a phrase or a metaphor, it actually contains very deep wisdom that not only helps us through difficulties, but can also change our overall perspectives. Another way of looking at it is to have difficult setbacks that may cause harm but also contain the potential for a beneficial outcome. When your rainbow does not have a silver lining, you need to shift your perspective to look at obstacles and challenges as opportunities to develop new qualities and improve your character. Just as diamonds are produced under pressure, you too can discover new capabilities and potential within yourself when you are placed under stress, which is the perspective of looking at a glass that is half full. We are sitting on a pot of gold, so instead of focusing on what we don't have, we should treasure the things we have. We may not always find a physical reward, but we can find a list of blessings that we can smile about.

Acknowledge what you can control, and let go of what you cannot. In the Bible, Noah and the inhabitants of the Ark were given hope through the sign of a rainbow, and it is still relevant today. It is important to avoid overusing this phrase when interacting with people that are experiencing challenges. Many trauma survivors may feel that other people are trivializing their bad news by saying that every cloud has a silver lining. We can fix this by being more sympathetic or empathetic. Many people are not trained to use good judgement when dealing with someone that may have encountered misfortune. Misfortune often serves as a catalyst for better things to happen, such as finding a new job or a better relationship after the loss of the old one. It is a helpful reminder to try to look for the positive rather than dwelling insistently on the negative in any situation.

When happens when the silver lining is not what you expected? Sometimes we have preconceived ideas of the expected outcome of a situation, before it is resolved. When the outcome is different, we may become disappointed, but God will always work things out in the way he sees fit. A silver lining in any form is better than none. With all the tragedies happening around the world due to COVID-19, many people are quickly forgetting how to be happy. Happiness that was once wrapped up in outer entertainment, has been replaced with silence and a new way of coping. We must be reminded that happiness is the perfect ingredient of successful coping during this crisis. We must find ways of creating small bits of solitude and happiness every day; it will go a long way in elevating our thoughts.

We can do a lot to create our own silver lining by living the lives that God expects from us. During this lockdown, you can work on strengthening your connections by spending quality time with your loved ones. Furthermore, since most people are now home from work, it is a good time to hug your kids, and spend more time at the dinner table having meaningful conversations. This would help in promoting and boosting oxytocin, which is a hormone that bonds people and has a calming effect on your body. The most important thing we should endeavor to do is to take charge of our mental health and come out of this experience stronger. We can do a lot to work on changing our brain chemistry. Positive emotions are a key resource for us during this pandemic crisis, because they can do a number of things to alter our perspectives.

> *"Nothing is predestined:*
> *The obstacles of your past can become*
> *the gateways that lead to new beginnings."*
> – Ralph Blum

Live Like the World Has No Sympathy for Your Weaknesses

I had to make the tough decision to stop feeling sorry for myself, and to move forward. The world is not that empathic to our weaknesses, so we cannot go around expecting society to make life easier for trauma survivors. I had the wrong perception, after my trauma experience. I thought that people would give me an easy time once they were aware of my past. I was basically piggybacking on my experience and trying to find an easy way out. Guess what? It did not work. We are living in a time in earth's history where people are caught up in the rat race, and many families are dysfunctional due to parents having two or more jobs. If you cannot motivate yourself to work on building your inner strength, then surely you will be disappointed. Even if you choose to disclose your dark past, the majority of people really don't care. It is not because they are bad people, but rather they are lacking the empathy to share the pain of others. It is easier to falsify a persona to the world than what we are experiencing inside. Many individuals may weigh the pros and cons of sharing their true feelings, depending on what they expect in each set of circumstances.

I am very good at hiding my true feelings, especially if it is something that would paint a different picture of the perceptions that others have of me. Let's be real: Our outer self is what we present to the world, so we usually try to curate it to reflect the best. This can become a huge problem because it can form habitual patterns at the expense of your true feelings. After my trauma, I buried my feelings because I did not want people to see how much it was affecting me. This went on for a while until, like a volcano, everything erupted, and my emotions went to Mars and back. I was an emotional wreck!! It was not until I solicited help from a professional, and opened up about my situation, that my life changed for the better. I had to learn that the natural response to pain is to run and hide away from the world because we are afraid of being judged. Today, I am no longer afraid to share my story. I have developed the mentality that I can expose my ugly side, and you can choose to take it or leave it. I am already a winner in my eyes, so I do not need to seek validation from others. To own your weaknesses, but not allow any growth to come from them, is like receiving the best gift in the world and refusing to open it.

We tend to focus more on our weaknesses than our strengths. I can recall when I was in a self-improvement group with many women, and we had an ice-breaker where we had to list our strengths and weaknesses. Many individuals had problems finding their strengths but had a long list of things that they were not good at. Do not let your weaknesses become your liability. You have a precious gift to share to the world, and your experience can become an asset. The world may not be as forgiving, but the most important person to decide your future is YOU. Weaknesses are a part of our lived experiences, and this may just change the sailing of your boat and charter it into deeper and more purposeful waters. I know that my experience played an integral part in my decision to seek further studies in a field that was relevant to my experience.

Our most important job is to leave an impact on the world, by leaving a legacy that will be a better version than what it was. Life may not be kind to us in one way or another, but we should find ways to utilize the little things every day that can positively impact the lives of others. Weakness reminds us that our lives are but a vapor, and that all flesh is like grass. We are reminded that God provides each breath to our lungs, and each beat to our hearts. He has numbered our days. He is the creator that upholds all things—even our puny, little, magnificent lives—by the word of his power. Seek God in your weakest state, because he is the potter, and he specializes in putting broken pieces together and making you a better version of yourself.

Trauma Survivors Are Not Damaged Goods

One of the biggest fears for me after trauma was the fear of not belonging or being accepted by society. There is a certain stigma that follows survivors and can be compared to a dark cloud hovering over your head. The fear of disclosing my experience was just as difficult as going through the trauma. Every time my experience was disclosed, there was a high possibility of being re-traumatized. That is why it is imperative to do so in a safe place, where you can get some form of emotional support, or when you are emotionally strong enough to handle the aftermath. We are not damaged goods; we have a story to tell that will charter the course for many other individuals as well, and will bring comfort and hope to many who are feeling hopeless and discouraged. Never underestimate the real power in sharing your story.

You do not have to carry the shame; that belongs to the abuser. For many years, my trauma kept me from uttering the truth about my past, and I did not want to take ownership of it. I felt that it was someone else's experience, and that I was too good a person for something this terrible to happen to. Once I stopped judging myself for what happened to me, the path to healing appeared clearer. I felt that the person inside of me deserved a safe, supportive place to heal, but first I had to make a decision to accept and not judge. Once I could understand this, telling my story became less triggering. Society may perceive trauma survivors as damaged, but the major player to determine who you are is you!! In the world, objects are meant to be built and then broken. The natural law of life is to constantly revolve, so it is expected that deterioration and death will take place; this process cannot be reversed. However, our souls can never be permanently damaged. They may encounter many obstacles that can slow the pace of progress, but there are always many ways to bounce back.

Trauma only impedes the way we function temporarily. Underneath all that pain is a soul waiting to be freed, and only you have that power to set yourself free from the shackles of the past. Do not get discouraged if you feel like "damaged goods." Use it to motivate yourself, and allow that feeling to transcend and find the true you. The famous sculptor, Michelangelo, explained how he could sculpt such beautiful angels in marble: *"I saw the angel in the marble, so I carved and carved and set her free."* Life's trials can wear us down. We are enchained in the loss, pain, and wounds of trauma, and it is hard to get it out of our psyches. Like Michelangelo, our souls get entangled and trapped in marble, but their effects go only as far as our perception and feelings allow them to go. Do not allow the circumstances of the past to affect the core of who you are. Change your perception, and you will evoke a change in your world that can reap long-term dividends.

Accessing professional help after trauma was very difficult for me, and it was even more challenging to find someone who believed in me. For many professionals, I was just another number that was added to their list of clients to help. I felt like a burden, so I resorted to my only place of comfort. As a social worker, I have learned from that experience to truly be accountable to my clients, and to always use a strength-based approach when clients are disclosing pertinent information. When trauma survivors are sharing information that is revealing a part of themselves that they have hid away from the world, even to themselves, it is imperative to have the necessary tools to perform damage control.

> *"Anything that is human is mentionable,*
> *and anything that is mentionable can be more manageable.*
> *When we talk about our feelings, they become less overwhelming,*
> *less upsetting, and less scary. The people we trust with*
> *that important talk can help us know we are not alone."*
> – Fred Rogers

What You Can Learn from Your Trauma

When I was a child, I thought I had all the time in the world; in fact, I was of the opinion that time was at a standstill. When I became older and started a family, time was going way too fast, and the hours in the day were just not enough. For many trauma survivors, the road to recovery is a long one; however, because we may believe that it is a long road ahead, we can remain stagnant for a long time. We may subconsciously derive comfort by indulging in habits such as self-pity and self-blame, which can lead to self-sabotage. Yes, time is the best healer for pain, but we must be careful not to prolong the healing process because we feel stuck and are thinking that we have all the time in the world. The longer you put off healing the more detrimental it might be for your overall health. See this horrifying event, which could leave a lifetime of memories, as an opportunity to heal and start afresh. Our characters are formed when we have been tried in the fire of life's circumstances and did not break; but instead, we came out stronger and more resilient.

We must use trauma as a means of growing, instead of reliving the past events. We need to create outlets where we can free our minds from the long-term bondage of any external control. Time can be your friend, or your greatest enemy where you can hold onto past hurts for a long time, and this can serve as a coping mechanism for many. As I mentioned in an earlier chapter, I was stuck for many years because I was holding onto the scars of the past. I would rehearse it at any given moment because I felt that I had a reason for being stagnant. This was a shield that I wore proudly, because it justified my actions, or lack thereof. Over time, my health was severely affected, and it was at this juncture that I had to make a decision to let it go so that I could be healthy. In addition, I had the wrong opinion of "letting go." I had the notion that letting go meant that I was telling the perpetrator that what they did was okay. It was later that I realized that I was giving myself permission to heal and become a better version of myself.

It is through life's most difficult circumstances that we become aware of our strengths. As a trauma survivor, I was not giving myself enough credit for the progress I was making in the personal growth department. After practicing self-praise, over time, I had a renewed sense of purpose. I used the darkest moment of my life to help others, and thus helped in healing myself. I utilized every connection during my years as a volunteer, and took it top notch in sharing my experience of trauma with others. What I learned was that there are many people who are hurting and have been digging their own graves while they are still alive. Their existence is based on showing others a part of themselves while they keep their past hidden. To heal, we must expose our vulnerabilities, even to ourselves. We need to admit that we are not okay, and that we are in need of help. You see, it is easy to wait until we feel whole before we reach out to others, but we can use our brokenness to help patch the pieces of the puzzle together for others, while healing ourselves. I found that in reaching out to others, I became more humble and grateful, and it created an outlet to start the process of healing. Experiencing trauma connects us firsthand with many countless individuals that have walked the same path as us, and they are the most selfless people you will ever meet. Once you are willing to relieve yourself of the burden of self-blame, and connect, then that connection and compassion is reciprocated to us and can provide a further source of strength.

Escaping Ugly

*"Give yourself time to heal from
a challenge you have been dealt.
Letting go of hurt does not happen overnight.
It happens in slow, small steps forward
(plus a few steps backwards at times).
Be gentle and patient with yourself."*
– Karen Salmansohn

Chapter 9

Avoid Familiarity and Opt for Change in Any Relationships

Whenever we are trying to break free from something or someone, we need to be willing to clear the path from past hurts, while trying to embrace something new. Trauma affects everyone, from various backgrounds. Managing the ongoing pain, for many trauma survivors, is a vital part of helping with the loss, grief, and pain of trauma. Let go of the pain rather than fight it. Many have resorted to focusing their energies on letting the pain become a secondary part of their lives, rather than the primary focus. Whatever way you decide to channel your focus, it is not an occasional process, but rather a lifelong process. Pain clouds one's judgement and affects the way we interact with those around us. It also causes us to make wrong judgements in relationships. Be mindful when you are choosing relationships in the future.

I am amazed at the beauty of nature. We are now experiencing fall, and I see it as a bittersweet moment because summer is over, and whether I like it or not, nature must continue. This is the same with trauma and pain. The process of life is not for us to choose, because God is the only one who is in control of nature and life. Gravitating to things that are familiar is natural because the place of comfort is something we use to fall back on when life get too difficult or stressful. However, that can be the very place that keeps us stuck or stagnant in our growth. Opting for change is not a bad thing; in fact, it can become your greatest blessing. The change in the seasons is a reminder that after winter comes spring. There are moments when it seems like the pain of trauma will never go away, but your season is coming where you will be reminded that better days are ahead. Just trust the process, and make wise decisions that will pay off in the end.

The moment that trauma takes place, we are wired with survival mechanisms that mobilize special resources for coping. There are many components that usually show up after trauma, such as determination, persistence, and courage, and these act as survival tools in a survivor's guide, during and after trauma. I have made many wrong decisions because of my past trauma, but I have learned to forgive myself and keep moving forward. Notwithstanding my past trauma, I count it as a privilege, because I am a better person due to my experience. My greatest asset is my willingness to embrace change; it is not as scary as many believe it to be. It is everyone's hope to escape the worst that life has to offer, but the strongest and most resilient among us use their most difficult challenges to propel themselves into something greater than their former state. Trauma can become a powerful point for change.

You Are Good Enough

The word "trauma" is a derivative of the Greek word for "wound." The term encompasses physical, psychological, and emotional ordeals. Any type of trauma can interfere with the daily functioning of a person's life, sometimes to a severe degree. In the early stages after trauma, my life was like a broken record. My life would usually follow a series of repetitive actions, where I would repeat phrases over and over as a means of strengthening my broken interior. These phrases and affirmations helped in building my self-esteem and motivation, and reiterated the point that I am good enough. There are many things I had to relearn because I felt robbed of the freedom to live the beautiful life that I had envisioned for myself. Many people who are not trauma survivors fail to see the deep devastation that trauma can have on an individual's life. It's sad to say that only those who feel it, know how deep these wounds can be, and the long-term effects it can have on an individual's life. Saying that you are good enough can act as a counteraction to shield the negative thoughts that attack you on a daily basis.

Trauma can cause our conscious minds to believe lies about ourselves and the world around us. It may tell us that loving ourselves is impossible, that peace is an illusion, and the worst yet, that things will never get better. It is easy to believe the lies because we have been brainwashed into believing them. Elie Wiesel, a holocaust survivor, gives an incredible account of the horror he experienced in a death camp in Auschwitz, Germany. He recounts some of the most horrifying events, which scarred him for a lifetime and marked the beginning of the end. It was while he was in the death camp and close to death that he decided to keep hope alive by using self-affirmations, and dreaming of a world of freedom outside of his present existence. Hope is the fuel that charted the course for Elie Wiesel, and it is something that was also instrumental in my journey. Elie went on to become one of the most humble and celebrated individuals, for his humanitarian efforts. He received the Noble Peace Prize in 1986, for speaking out against violence, repression, and racism.

Trauma is not a death sentence; it can serve as a turning point in our experience. It can lead you to a new career path and act as a catalyst in changing the course of your destiny for good. Everything depends on how we perceive our experiences, and how willing we are to not stay a victim but be a victor. I became an advocate against issues of violence, incest, and abuse after my trauma. As I mentioned in an earlier chapter, I was motivated to change my career path and pursue a career I was passionate about, one where I could use my experience of trauma to help others. It would not have been possible if I hadn't learned how to love myself and develop an attitude of refusing to lie down and play dead. The world is full of possibilities, and we can use our experiences to helped change the world. Were it not for my past, my future would have looked completely different. Give yourself permission to not only think you are good enough, but most importantly, to truly believe you are.

The famous Mark Twain coined these words: *"Twenty years from now, you will be more disappointed by the things that you didn't do than by the ones you did do. So throw off the bowlines. Sail away from safe harbor. Catch the trade winds in your sails. Explore. Dream. Discover."* You have the capacity to overcome trauma and live the life you have always wanted. You are good enough!! Never waste another day feeling sorry for yourself. History is a prerequisite to teach us that many successful individuals experienced the worst living conditions, yet went on to become powerful and successful individuals in society. You once gave up your power by believing you did not have any; don't make the same mistake twice. Second chances are meant to build a strong foundation, not cripple the spark of hope for betterment.

Personal Development

People have a tendency to gravitate toward the latest technological devices, and may upgrade their handsets, cars, etc. every year. Individuals love the smell of something new, and feel unaccepted by their peers if they are not sporting the newest devices on the market. I once had someone call me old-fashioned for having what they called an outdated phone. My concept has always been that if something is not broken, don't fix or replace it. We are not programmed to invest in ourselves; it is something we need to intentionally set out to do. Personal development is not on the to-do lists of the majority of people. We weren't taught how to invest in ourselves, so we can't crucify ourselves for something we were never taught. When we invest in ourselves, our value increases, and so we become more marketable and a huge asset to ourselves. You can never get out of life more than you are worth. If other people are not seeing your worth, then it is time to do self-introspection and check what you are selling. Whatever we are selling, that is what people buy into.

Personal development becomes even more relevant in your life when you have encountered a traumatic event of any proportion. The idea of personal development is to guide you toward living a better and more rewarding life. Many people have no idea what personal development is, so having a plan for this topic may seem difficult. It is something we must strive to understand and implement in our lives, because life itself is a continuous learning progress. If you ignore it and don't consciously embark on a plan to improve your life, you may wake up one day to the reality that you are living a life that you are not pleased with, and by then, it may be too late to make a change. If 2020 taught us anything, it is that life is too short to prolong not living your best life. We need to appreciate each moment and make it count. Many times, we are afraid of change because we do not want anything that may threaten our comfort zones; we want change but do not want to put in the work.

Trauma can weaken our strength, so it is imperative to embark on a plan to build up our strength. One way of doing this is personal development. When you take time to focus on nurturing and using your strengths, you will see significant improvement in your life. You also create opportunities to develop your skills by developing a positive asset search to find things you are already good at. When you make the decision to improve your skills, it takes you a step closer to feeling more confident. Personal development can serve as a road map in helping you to achieve your goals and boost your confidence. In the journey of personal development, we are constantly learning new things about ourselves, and it also creates space where we can grow and improve our lives. Personal development can help you in all areas of your life, and it is therefore largely a personal journey, but one that needs to be prioritised. The benefits are that you grow as a person while growing your skills, you improve your self-awareness, and you boost your confidence. Abraham Maslow once said, *"You can either step forward into growth or step backwards into safety."* We hold the keys to our lives, and the process of becoming is in our grips. We either work on becoming a better version of ourselves or we spiral downwards into the crevices of our narrow existence. Since life is growth, if we stop growing spiritually or emotionally, then we are as good as dead.

Counteracting Feelings of Worthlessness

For years, I was stuck in the blaming game; I felt that something was wrong with me, and that I was the reason why all these bad things happened in the first place. Since birth, I was told that I was a miracle baby, and I was also told some really bad things as well. For example, I was the only child born at home, and I can recall a family member saying that if I hadn't been born at home, they would have thought I didn't belong to the family. Furthermore, I was verbally, physically, and sexually abused, and this was ignored for a long time. In the Caribbean culture, adults are seen as always being right, and their actions are justified even if it crosses the borders of the worst kind of crimes. Furthermore, even insinuating that an adult did something inappropriate was not tolerated, and a child would be automatically disqualified and punished for saying it. I felt lost in a world where the adults dominated and called the shots, while I had to suffer years of abuse. I cannot fully explain the feelings of unworthiness and neglect that I suffered, and how this could have led me to a path of destruction and even suicide. Can you imagine your grandmother—a person who is supposed to protect you—being a part of your early undoing by allowing such atrocities to happen under her watch?

Because I was brainwashed into believing that I was not good enough, I automatically attracted bad situations/relationships into my life. I did not have the awareness of the methods to use for counteracting negative emotions. I was one sad, depressed child/teenager, and no one took notice of my plight. It was not until my mother intervened, when I was a teenager, that I was finally freed from the bondage of abuse. I thought my freedom would last forever, but unfortunately, I had an encounter that almost destroyed my sanity. Life for me was never a bed of roses, and I truly can say that I did not get the opportunity to enjoy my childhood. Counteracting feelings of worthlessness during and after trauma can be difficult; however, it is possible. One can feel like a puzzle with some missing pieces, but we can find wholeness by digging deep into our souls. Feelings of worthlessness can leave you feeling insignificant and useless, and these feelings may develop into a prolonged state of negative mood, and if not monitored, can affect one's physical and mental health. The effects of trauma can cause people to create a false self of who they are, and it is easy to believe the negative voices. Whether you witnessed or experienced violence as a child, or your caretakers emotionally or physically neglected you, when you grow up in a traumatizing environment, you are likely to still show signs of trauma as an adult.

Trauma is something that one cannot easily erase, since it shapes and forms our characters and behaviors, but we have the power to choose what we become. When one's feelings of worthlessness go unaddressed, they may rapidly become overwhelming and interfere significantly with the ability to function. It may be difficult to cope with these feelings without professional help, and when worthlessness occurs as a symptom of depression or any mental health condition other than immediate crisis, therapy is often beneficial. Facing the problems that worthlessness has created in your life can be daunting. You may be overwhelmed with the problem of how to heal the shame caused by the childhood abuse you experienced. The good news is that there is a way to heal your feelings of worthlessness so that you can begin to see the world through different eyes—eyes that are not clouded by the perception that you are less than, inadequate, damaged, or unlovable. You are a rare kind, and your experience of trauma should be used to make you a better individual.

> *"We have been made to feel less than worthy, a lot of the time to feel worthless, and do you know why? Because we listened. We listened to what other people had to say about us, but we forgot to listen to the person that truly matters: our self."*
> – Steven Aitchison

Make Your Latter Greater

There is absolutely no denying that trauma can change us, but it also helps us to grow. On August 28, 2009, Whitney Houston made a huge comeback on the music charts with her song, "Didn't Know My Own Strength." The lyrics touched every part of me and spoke volumes as to Whitney's struggle to get back on her feet. Many survivors of trauma and others alike can identify with this song. It is only when we are tried in the fire of life that we become aware of our strength, since nothing confirms our strengths like weathering major adversities. I have learned so much from my experience, for it was my darkest moments that helped spur me on to help others. As a survivor of childhood abuse, I am an advocate for the marginalized. It is my aim to strive to bring goodness to the world, recognizing that there is already enough suffering and hate. The childhoods of many have been robbed; children are traumatized and are without a voice. Many are neglected, and the adults cease to take notice of their plight. My abuse went on for years without any adult intervention.

I have learned a lot over the years from my experience with trauma. It was awful, and scary at times, but I have learned to value life more than before. Life can be a bit of a paradox, and can appear less appealing after a traumatic experience. The human brain is always searching for meaning; we have inherited a strong inclination to want to understand our experiences. I had a narrative of the kind of life I wanted, and everything went totally contrary to what I envisioned. Trying to find meaning and hope through something so awful and unfair can be very difficult, but meaning will come with TIME. From my own experience, one way of coping was to adopt the mindset of finding the good in the bad.

Elie Wiesel found tremendous meaning through his experience at the Nazi concentration camps. He not only survived the horrors of the holocaust, but he also witnessed the death of his father, and was separated from his sister and mother, who later died. Through his experience, it would have been easy for him to wallow in despair, but he made up his mind that despair was not an option. If you have been through trauma, like most of us have, you may recognize in yourself the ways you have grown through your trauma. Or perhaps you are not at that place yet, but no matter where you are in your experience, growth is not something you can force. Neither is there a timeline you can set to heal; this is a lifetime work that requires small steps, one day at a time. Premature attempts to completely heal or to make ourselves feel a particular way about the trauma, can be a failure. We are a work in progress.

As a trauma survivor, I have learned not to blame myself for what happened. Instead of blaming or becoming angry with myself, I am more compassionate and forgiving toward myself. Although reactions such as anger, guilt, anxiety, and depression are completely normal after trauma, these would only make things more difficult. Trauma may have interrupted the plot and changed the narrative of the way I wanted my life to go, but I count myself blessed to have been chosen to live this life. God still holds the blueprint of our lives in his hands, and at every turn, whether good or bad, he is the holder of the narratives for our lives, not us. My dependence on God has deepened as a result of my experience with trauma, because when I didn't have anyone to turn to for comfort, He was there, and He is still a pivotal part of my experience.

> *"There are wounds that never show on the body that are deeper and more hurtful than anything that bleeds."*
> – Laurell K. Hamilton

Retraumatization (What to Do)

Retraumatization is a conscious or unconscious reminder of past trauma that results in a re-experiencing of the initial traumatic event. It can be triggered by a situation, an attitude, or expression, or by certain environments that replicate the dynamics (loss of power/control or safety) of the original trauma. Furthermore, people can also re-experience their own trauma through other people's ordeals. For me, I was retraumatized through the experience of a close family member. This resurfaced my own trauma, and I had to help my family member through their traumatic experience. Some of my old scars that were buried years ago, came to the forefront, and it became even more difficult to cope. I was later diagnosed with PTSD. My success getting through PTSD was to not allow the label to take dominance over my life. I have the power to speak into every diagnosis, and claim the things that I want in order to effect positive change. I am not my trauma; I had to learn to separate myself from the ugly side of my life, which I had absolutely no control over.

Retraumatization can leave many survivors feeling more vulnerable, suicidal, and disenfranchised from society. I recently read the heart-wrenching story of Catherine "Daisy" Coleman, a rape survivor whose story was told in the 2016 Netflix documentary, *Audrie & Daisy*, and who was a co-founder of the comprehensive SafeBAE (Safe Before Anyone Else), which focuses on ending sexual assault among middle and high school students. She died by suicide at age 23. Audrie Taylor Pott also took her own life, in 2012, at age 15. Why were these two young and promising lives cut short by suicide? It was reported that for one victim, she was traumatized after sharing her story.

When I decided to share my story for the first time, I felt like I was reliving the entire experience, along with that of my family member. I did not have a support system in place to bear the brunt of such catastrophic information, so I was tossed into a whirlwind that was blowing out of control. I did not realize that I had just opened a box of information from which I had absolutely no idea how to move forward. My therapist at that time tried her best, but she didn't have the answers to soothe my chaotic life.

After I completed my studies in social work, I understood the importance of adopting a strength-based approach, and that to avoid retraumatization, it is vital to adopt a trauma-informed approach when working with clients. It is also imperative to do a positive asset search to help in building individuals up, who are disclosing their lived experiences. If a professional is not equipped with the tools necessary to build a relationship with clients, to allow them to disclose information when they are ready, the damage can be even more detrimental, and can lead to retraumatization. Remember that each individual needs a cushion to bounce back from after unloading the burdens they have been carrying for years. It risks reopening old wounds and ingraining the old emotional reactions that happened at the time of the original trauma. The process of retraumatization can occur while talking about it, so it is necessary to create a plan to deal with your triggers. One can learn ways of counteracting triggers that can result in retraumatization; however, we may lose some battles on the journey of healing, and that is expected. Trauma victims cannot recover until they become familiar with and befriend the sensations in their bodies. You cannot disassociate yourself from your trauma; there is a need to embrace the past scars before one can move forward. For change to take place, we should reacquaint ourselves with our bodies and how they interact with the world around us. Physical awareness is the first step in releasing the tyranny of the past.

Notes

Chapter 10

Trauma Recovery

Recovery is the ultimate goal in the process of your experience with trauma. It doesn't necessarily mean total freedom from the past. There will be many times when you feel like a lone vessel surrounded by a large mass of water. When many individuals think about trauma, it is natural to focus only on certain situations or events, and to label them as traumatic. For example, a car accident, war, sexual abuse, or natural disasters. However, trauma can take many forms. One example of this is narcissistic abuse. It is one of the most popular forms of trauma; however, many people do not speak about it. Why is this so? It is a soul-crushing form of trauma because it slowly builds up like an avalanche. It is very subtle and can start off as a loving relationship, with the individual becoming controlling and dominating over time. Typically, a narcissist does not take responsibility for their behavior, and shifts the blame to others. When you try to highlight their faults, you are viewed as the one with the problem. Some narcissists are not capable of feeling guilt, and have issues with doing self-reflection. Healing from this type of trauma can be even more difficult, since it is an ongoing process and not an instantaneous event.

Any form of trauma can leave you feeling hopeless, useless, and empty; it robs you of your strength and can render you incapable of articulating your true feelings. Working through the process of trauma recovery is crucial and may look different for many. For me, in the initial stage of trauma, I thought I would never experience the meaning of true happiness. What I learned is that happiness starts within, and even if outside factors are working against me, I have the power of choice in determining the outcome. In order to heal from trauma, there needs to be an acknowledgment, accountability, and an agreement with yourself. Too many times, we want to heal without laying down the foundation for the healing process to take place. If you want to thrive, you must be willing put in the work and ride the roller coaster, with all the ups and downs that come with it. Be responsible for your own growth, and take notes of every victory or setback while learning to roll with the punches that life throws at you.

The process of trauma recovery is not referring to recovering what was stolen from the victim. We can never get back what was lost; however, we can learn new strategies in closing that chapter of our lives, and become the captain of our ships by taking back control of our bodies. In the beginning of your trauma, you were a victim, but you can't stay in that stage forever. As you progress through trauma, you will want to reach the stage where you can empower others. To serve and empower others can be the final stage in your trauma recovery. It doesn't necessarily mean that you forget about your trauma, or that it doesn't affect you anymore. What it does mean is that even if you are triggered by external stimuli, you can see this ahead of time and decipher what course of action to take. Your experience should serve as a means of helping others.

Healing is like an onion. As you progress through one layer of trauma to release the pain and heal, a new layer will surface. One layer after another will bring up new issues to focus on. It is imperative that you focus on one layer at a time. The wounds can only become giants based on how you feel them. Refocus and restructure your energy, while adopting the frame of mind that every victory is forming blocks that can lead to the path of healing. On the road to trauma recovery, you should not be afraid to name your emotions, become vigilant, and safeguard your emotional well-being. Acknowledge everything you are feeling, and learn to let go by visualizing the energy of the trauma slowly leaving your body. Another example of what was effective for me was to write a letter to someone that hurt me, and place it in a tub of water and slowly watch it dissolve. You are a walking miracle, ready to be elevated to the true purpose of your existence.

Gifts Hide Under the Layers of Grief

We need to learn to endure our crucible moments: times in our lives when we experience circumstances that forever transform us. They may even challenge one to question their beliefs and values, and leave one with a completely new identity, which often refers to a place of testing. Every challenge forces us to seek to find meaning, which can lead us to become more teachable, open-minded, and adaptable, where resiliency resides and leads one to search for a new identity. The natural tendency is to disassociate from the trauma, not realizing that it is better to rebuild on the old foundation and embrace all of your scars. We can never fathom our hidden strengths unless we are tried in the fire of life. As we encounter trials, it not only builds our character, but we gather many survival skills that equip us for any difficulties we will encounter on our life's journey.

We are living in a time where distress and sadness is the order of the day. Over the years, we have experienced many disasters—we lived through 9/11 and Hurricane Sandy, for example—but nothing could have prepared us for COVID-19. The collective trauma that the world is experiencing is the biggest tragedy to ever hit the world, and with every passing day, more extraordinary sadness comes with it. In every tragedy, there are opportunities for transformation, as we learn to not only endure but also to grow from these experiences. A crucible is a vessel used for refining metals. It is often used as a metaphor for trials. In the natural sense, when we think about trials, we tend to see them in a negative way; however, as Christians, we can view them in the biblical frame of God's redemptive work. This view results in peace, contentment, and spiritual growth, instead of bitterness, anxiety, and stunted spiritual growth.

Crucibles can serve as life changing events that can catapult our lives into unknown territories, which can lead us to discover our true purposes. The story of Prince Harry is something that caught the world's attention and painted the picture of a young man who was out of touch with reality. For 20 years, he attempted to bury his grief, even using the honorable military service, and wild partying, as a way of coping with his loss. He had a hard time coping with the death of his mom, and resorted to ways of coping that would mark him as the out-of-control Prince of Wales. He hit rock bottom with the well-publicized nude photos of him partying in Las Vegas. Prince Harry learned the principle of reframing his crucibles by using the tragedy to embark on a path to recover his losses and transform his image.

We still have a lot of gifts to discover that are hidden under the blanket of pain and grief. Use every opportunity, when coping with grief in any form, to elevate your life and transform your thinking patterns. Look at Prince Harry today; he is a true example of what a transformed mind can accomplish. Many are waiting for lasting happiness, which is everything all of us are thriving for, but in order to enjoy the life we envision, we need to raise our game plan. When we choose to accept and embrace our adversities, we are opening doors to give ourselves permission to heal.

> *"Adversity is neither friend nor foe. It is a common acquaintance that is desired less and rewarded most when embraced."*
> – Carolyn Wells

Every Level Demands a New You

Every level demands a new you, and sometimes it takes being broken to reinvent yourself and discover a new you. One must be willing to implement change on every level to overcome the many challenges they encounter along life's journey. We all know that life is filled with ups and downs, but when you're in the midst of a particularly hard time, it can be hard to picture how you'll ever get out of it. In life, we develop ways of navigating challenges, and this can help us to develop a sense of confidence through our ability to cope. You cannot remain the same person and expect the next level of your life to become a reality. If you continue to make the same mistakes over and over, and make the same decisions, short of the more mature and informed ones needed for the next season, you will remain where you are. Your better and destined future will remain far-fetched.

Sometimes it is simply about growing up and learning from your mistakes... about having a moment and reflecting on your life; identifying and admitting the loopholes you have condoned; sacrificing the old you by leaving behind what makes you who you are now; and embracing a better and more mature thoughtful you, for your better tomorrow and your next level. The world's greatest sprinter, Carl Lewis, will always be remembered as the single most captivating sprinter the world of track and field has ever seen in the circuit of Olympic competition. He was always consistent and versatile, and always would win gold medals in his pursuits. He attributed his success, in and off the field, to a life devoted to harnessing his skills by consistently changing his game plan on every level, and gravitating to things that improve his performances daily.

A new you is needed when things change, and you have a choice to embrace the change or resist it. But it is imperative to note that with every decision, there are consequences, and either way can be just as successful as you want it to be. You can't expect success on every level if you refuse to change your tactics; you can either view change as a success or a challenge. I believe that many of us are afraid of it because it demands us to step out of our comfort zones and embrace something that we may consider bigger than ourselves. The problem is that many people never evolve; they are stuck in being who they are, and never explore the option of the many possibilities of who they can become. It is impossible to balance an empty glass in the same hand with a full glass. Leonardo DiCaprio once said, *"Every level of your life demands a different you."*

Instead of being satisfied with the same, stagnant, mediocre, and boring lives, we can trade this for success, contentment, and progress. The mind was made to expand and create growth; if the mind is not stretched to discover new experiences, then we can't reach new dimensions. The biggest problem is that we fail to exercise our minds, so they remain dormant and lazy. Everything in nature speaks of growth; it is only human nature that finds it difficult to make change a common practice. A different version of yourself is waiting on your next level. When you feel yourself changing, don't hold yourself back, and don't become fearful. Growing may appear difficult, but you will find that with every drop of tears or sweat you put in, you will become a different, better version of yourself, and the universe will take note and help you along the way. A different you is waiting on the horizon, and the next level is waiting for you to fulfill your God-given purpose.

Give Yourself the Keys to Your New Beginning

I can recall, years ago, a husband expressing his opinion to me, regarding his wife's addiction to shopping. As a result of this, they had frequent arguments, which resulted in years of financial strain on the family. Over time, it had taken its toll on their marriage, and eventually he had to give her an ultimatum: If she continued with this, he would walk out. Many people find it easy to gravitate to new things. They appear to experience an instant high when receiving a package and waiting to unveil the new smell. My friend's wife made the decision to change her bad habit, because it would have cost her the marriage. Trauma can make you feel like an old, discarded item, and waiting to feel fresh and new again seems like a farfetched dream. My friend's wife was trying to fill a void, and one of her coping mechanisms was shopping. What are some of the things you can do to cope? Experiencing trauma does not have to be the end of the road for you; instead, it can become your new beginning. My experience with trauma knocked me flat on my face, but I used the opportunity to reinvent myself and pursue some of the things I thought I could not. I learned to love myself, went back to school, and became a stronger, more resilient individual. I was the one calling the shots, and I chose to be happy and learned to enjoy my own company; but most importantly, silence was not that scary anymore, because I learned to make peace with my past.

When your first encounter with trauma happens, it takes your body and emotions to a level that you thought never existed. Due to lack of preparation, it feels like you were robbed of your most precious prized possession. Your emotions come at you all at once: You may feel rage at the perpetrator, fear that the perpetrator will return, hurt that someone took advantage of you, or embarrassed because you weren't prepared, or you may even grieve for the lost items after a robbery or disaster. Some of these will happen in phases, but they have the tendency to overlap and can overwhelm you easily. On June 18, 2009, a family member lost her husband to the cold hand of death. He returned home to recover something he needed for work that day, and an intruder murdered him. I will never forget that day, because my daughter was born that same day, and a friend got married. Looking back now, I marvel at how amazing God is: In one day, I experienced life, death, and a new beginning. We are privileged with the endless possibilities that life has in store for us, and it is just a matter of being positive and seeing miracles in every second of the day.

When I completed my studies in social work, my professors always emphasized the point that a new future awaits you out there. When we open our eyes every day, we are given fresh opportunities for a new start. You can picture the open highway stretched out to infinity before you, beckoning to a future somewhere out on that horizon, and taking you to an adventure. Our journey to becoming starts with what lies out there on the horizon and is waiting for you to discover. We only discover more when we are willing to push the limits beyond what we can see with our eyes, to what we feel in our gut. You see, sometimes the eyes can deceive us into believing that all of what we see is all there is, but once we are motivated to search for more, we will find it

As you open the doors to a new you, there should not be any room for regret. You have overcome the worst, and you are still standing. Use the keys you have been given to gift yourself new dimensions in your experience. Not everyone is as fortunate as you are, and not many understand what it means to be stripped of your dignity and still find a way to escape the crevices of your thoughts and emotions.

From Brokenness to Wholeness
– How to Paint Your Broken Pieces Gold

Everywhere we look around us, we do not have to look far to see how broken the world is. We see it in our churches, families, communities, and in individuals. We are quick to fix things that are broken, yet we neglect humanity. What do we do with broken people? When I say "brokenness," I am referring to any kind of loss, disappointment, or struggle. The Japanese have a method called "kintsugi." This is used for repairing broken ceramics, with a special lacquer mixed with gold or platinum. The philosophy behind the technique is to recognize the history of the object, and to visibly incorporate the repair into the new piece instead of disguising it. The attempt is not to hide the damage, but rather to illuminate the original damage. The process usually results in something more beautiful than the original. Brokenness does not mean the end; it can signal the beginning of something even more beautiful than what you have lost. When you are on the path to wholesomeness, it is expected that your brokenness will summon light into the deepest crevices of your heart. There is something beautiful about rising from the ashes after falling completely apart. It might sound crazy, but there is beauty in pain. Not all pain is bad—when you have rolled with the punches of life, you learn that some pain actually helps you to become stronger.

Truth be told, happiness is not the absence of problems but the ability to deal with them. Imagine all the wondrous things that your mind might embrace if it were not wrapped so tightly around your struggles. Brokenness can be one of your greatest blessings. When you are reflecting on your life, always look back on what you have now instead of what you have lost. It is not what the world takes away from you that counts; it is what you do with what you have left. Build on the things you have in the present, and count your blessings, for little is more when God is in it. Holding onto the past can be compared to drinking poison and expecting the target of your anger to die instead of you.

My brokenness was caused by those who were supposed to protect me. One of life's greatest joys can be connecting to another soul, in what may sometimes feel like a lonely world. A good relationship, especially with members of your household, can be a landing on which to fall when the inevitable pains of life strike—a safe harbor to point us in the direction of home when we feel lost. What happens when the hands that are supposed to protect you—the hands you rely on to soothe your pain in times of hardship—are the source of the very pain? My circle of protection became my biggest enemy, and the product of my undoing. How can the journey to wholeness take place when your environment, your safe haven, is hell on earth? When the agony of a broken heart feels like the stabbing of a thousand knives, how does one even begin the healing process?

Life places us in various positions and closes doors because it's time to move forward. And that's a good thing because we often won't move unless circumstances force us to. Pain creates a force within us that propels us to move forward from our pain and find our purpose. Move on from what hurts you, but never forget the lessons to be learned and what they taught you. Don't measure your progress based on your struggles; just because you are struggling doesn't mean you're failing. Every great success story requires some type of worthy struggle to get there. Many success stories start with many failures, but it is through perseverance and a heart that beats for something greater than your past, that will get you from brokenness to wholeness. Stay positive and patient; everything will come together—maybe not immediately, but eventually.

How to Move Forward after Trauma

There is a Chinese proverb: "The journey of a thousand miles starts with one step," which means that a person must begin his or her journey to reach their goal or destination. This serves as motivation that expresses deep insight about determination and avoiding procrastination. This expression can be instrumental in expressing to us that great things start with simple, intentional steps, which can in turn lead to a great path. I believe that we can all overcome our flaws and become the masterpieces of our generation. Moving forward is always a good thing; however, one cannot move forward blindly. A concrete plan needs to be in place, with some measure of accountability to self. Your thoughts can become your greatest enemy, so it is necessary to guard the avenue of your thoughts, because they do become actions. We are tossed onto an emotional roller coaster, and this emotional overwhelm is like that of a shaken bottle of soda. Inside the bottle is a tremendous amount of pressure. The safest way to release the pressure is to open and close the cap in a slow, cautious, and intentional manner to prevent an explosion.

Feeling stuck is common for trauma survivors, but it is imperative to keep an open mind to move forward. Maintaining your feelings of safety and stability should be on the forefront of the healing process. Once you figure out what makes you feel safe and what does not, then you are a notch higher in your life. In moving forward, you need to develop courage. Your willingness to heal from trauma will forge the path to making tough decisions that will develop your character. Moving past trauma, for many people, can feel like it is taking a lifetime. We must move away from what the mind is saying; it can act as a protective mechanism because it may not be ready to process certain information. Furthermore, the mind may want to stay in the safe zone, which does not require the strain of trying to resolve the problem or even find solutions.

There was once a part of you that felt disenfranchised from society; you were stuck in a bubble of self-doubt, and silenced by your inner turmoil. You were once stuck in a bubble where the emphasis was on self and healing the wounded soul, but now, to put your best foot forward, you need to reintegrate yourself into society. It is a form of a rebranding process, where you are preparing yourself for becoming a new improved you. It is taking the past trauma and accepting it as a part of your past. The best thing you can do for yourself is to learn from it, re-evaluate, and compare yourself to who you were then and who you are now. Walk with confidence into a new stage of your life; you have made it, you have survived, and you can share your growth by giving others the opportunity to learn and grow from it as well. People are waiting to hear your story of survival and growth; you can become a spark of light to brighten the dark path for many who are without hope. Your story is not for you only but for the world. Live a little better every day, and make improvements as you go along.

> *"Inaction is the killer of many dreams and good intentions."*
> – Deloris Gardner

You are failing yourself when you fail to infuse your life with action. Do not wait for it to happen—rather, make it happen. We are all destined for greatness, but we must be willing to put in the work, with hope of a better future. Keep hope alive; treat the past as a lesson, the present as a gift, and the future as your motivation. Every day above ground is truly a gift from God. Every day creates new opportunities for hope, growth, and gratitude to our creator. Sometimes we have the notion that moving forward entails having everything figured out. You will never be in a place where everything is perfect, but you can work with the little you have and build on that. Do not make the mistake of taking things that are meant to be in the past, and trying to carry them into your future. Know when something has ended. Shutting doors, closing certain chapters... whatever you choose to call it, what is important is to leave things in the past and move forward.

Notes

About the Author

Deloris C Gardner is a first-time author. She is a social worker by profession, and an advocate for social justice. She was instrumental in the establishment of the first Weston Tenant Association, for which she serves as the chairperson. She is very involved in community work and has served as volunteer for various community projects, including the Mission of Hope outreach program, COSTI Senior's Craft program and Mount Dennis Community Care program. The idea for her book *Escaping Ugly: How to Overcome Trauma and Moving from Surviving to Thriving* came because of her own personal experience as a survivor of childhood abuse. If you have ever experienced any form of trauma and are finding it difficult to cope, this book will take you in-depth and give you simple steps to guide you on the road to recovery. From an early age, Deloris has always been fascinated by words and books. She can recall sitting in a banana field in her home country and envisioning a life outside of a once narrow existence. We can become products of our environment by choice. Deloris made the choice a long time ago to dream, and block out anything and anyone that keeps her from doing so.

Her life did a 180 degree turn when she read the book *Think and Grow Rich* by Napoleon Hill. This book formed the catalyst of her vision to become a published writer, and help her to realize that she could achieve anything in life. Furthermore, she became mindful to guard her thoughts, but even deeper she developed the understanding that she has the power to decipher what she allows to dominate her life.

Escaping Ugly

Trauma can leave many survivors feeling disenfranchised from society; it can also leave them feeling very lost. When Deloris started on her journey of recovery it was not an easy task; however, she made the decision to change the course of her life by guarding her thoughts. It is her hope that everyone who reads this book will embrace it with an open mind, to let go of the past and forge a new path forward into the unknown. Trauma is not an end but can be a beginning that can open the door to many possibilities.

www.ingramcontent.com/pod-product-compliance
Lightning Source LLC
Chambersburg PA
CBHW070920150426
43193CB00011B/1532